A WOMAN'S INFLUENCE

ALSO BY TONY A. GASKINS JR.

Make It Work

A WOMAN'S INFLUENCE

Own Your *WORTH*, Cultivate Your *POWER*, and
Change Your *RELATIONSHIPS* for the Better

TONY A. GASKINS JR.
SHERI GASKINS

HOWARD BOOKS

ATRIA

New York   London   Toronto   Sydney   New Delhi

HOWARD
B O O K S

ATRIA

An Imprint of Simon & Schuster, Inc.
1230 Avenue of the Americas
New York, NY 10020

First Howard Books/Atria Paperback edition April 2021

HOWARD BOOKS/ATRIA PAPERBACK and colophon
are trademarks of Simon & Schuster, Inc.

For information about special discounts for bulk purchases, please contact Simon & Schuster Special Sales at 1-866-506-1949 or business@simonandschuster.com.

The Simon & Schuster Speakers Bureau can bring authors to your live event. For more information or to book an event, contact the Simon & Schuster Speakers Bureau at 1-866-248-3049 or visit our website at www.simonspeakers.com.

Interior design by Jill Putorti

Manufactured in the United States of America

3 5 7 9 10 8 6 4 2

Library of Congress Cataloging-in-Publication Data

Names: Gaskins, Tony A., author. | Gaskins, Sheri, author.
Title: A woman's influence : own your worth, cultivate your power, and change your relationships for the better / Tony A. Gaskins Jr., Sheri Gaskins.
Description: New York : Howard Books, 2020.
Identifiers: LCCN 2020000580 | ISBN 9781501199356 (hardcover) | ISBN 9781501199370 (ebook)
Subjects: LCSH: Man-woman relationships. | Relationship quality. | Sex role.
Classification: LCC HQ801 .G37 2020 | DDC 305.3—dc23
LC record available at https://lccn.loc.gov/2020000580

ISBN 978-1-5011-9935-6
ISBN 978-1-5011-9936-3 (pbk)
ISBN 978-1-5011-9937-0 (ebook)

CONTENTS

CONTENTS

A WOMAN'S INFLUENCE

INTRODUCTION

I've been on this journey since 2007. It started as me trying to right my wrongs. I'd been so many things to women, but always I had been less than the man I could have been. As luck or destiny would have it, I had saved the best of me for the woman who would become my wife. In other words, I met my match. There's an inexplicable desire in a man to settle for less than his best manhood. We take shortcuts in love and relationships but somehow expect grand results. I was no different.

Then I met this woman who'd had enough. I met her right after a toxic relationship I'd had. She'd gone through something similar. I wanted to play more games, and she was fed up with the games. Her tolerance for men's games was maxed out, and she was about business. Although she was only nineteen, she'd doubled her experience as if she were forty. Game, set, match. The days of her dealing with grown boys were over. She would require my best, but I wasn't aware of that in the beginning. It wasn't long before I found out.

We clicked immediately. Our first meet-up lasted six hours. When I got up off the bench, I had the imprint of the seat in my shorts because we'd sat so long discussing everything from sports to politics. Our hearts were yearning for real love, but only one of us knew the path to it. I wasn't the one who would guide us into eternal love, nor was I even a willing participant at times. I wanted love but not the work it takes to have it. Everyone says they want love, but not many want to do the work.

For more than twelve years now, I've taught on love, and so much of my knowledge was formed because of my relationship with my wife. Greater than any education, certification, or training is real-life experience. If you ask anyone from any field, they'll tell you there is no greater teacher than the experience. I've lived and I've loved at the highest level. I've gained lessons from my lower self and from my higher self. All lessons coincide, yet they all contradict. There's a flow and a balance when understanding real love. Certain lessons apply to certain moments, and another lesson may contradict the one you need in this moment. You have to know what's right for you—and what isn't.

I am so enthralled by love that I don't have any choice but to teach what I've learned. My wife isn't the same. She's more of a doer than a talker. She lives and lives fully. But I've been able to convince her to share some of what she's learned and some of what she's taught me along the way. I don't believe there are ample words for everything we've discovered, but this is our effort. I'm the one who loves writing about my journey. She's the one who loves living hers. In this book, I'm going to pour my heart out, and my wife will add her touches as she sees fit. There's something that tells me I'm still under her spell of feminine influence, and if she lists every ingredient, it will break the spell. This spell isn't magical; it's spiritual. It's deeper than we've ever gone in love, and we've noticed that not many have experienced it. It's not bondage; it's freedom. It's not sinful; it's righteous. It's not painful; it's blissful. There's no fantasy; it's all reality. Let us take you on this journey to understanding a woman's influence in a very real way.

Chapter 1

A MAN'S WORLD

From the White House to your house, we live with the world's reasoning that a man should lead without the influence of a woman. For thousands of years, women were suppressed to a life of being "barefoot and pregnant." I believed everything I was taught about women and everything I saw play out in the world around me. It all said that a man is the head and a woman is the tail. It's a man's world, and men have all the say in what happens. Millions of women believe the same thing. Although there's an uprising of women who are determined to shake things up, the majority of women I meet have suppressed their inner wisdom and greatness to assume a lesser role in life.

Most of the women I meet and see portrayed on television who are fighting against the system seem to be doing so from a place of anger and frustration. I can't blame them because I'm sure I'd be upset if the world had its foot on my neck and shackles on my feet. In a lot of ways, the fights of women and people of color are similar. Imagine the fight of a woman of color. That has to be the lowest position in the world, if we're being honest. To be born a certain race or to be born a woman are things beyond our control. Yet you have to suffer the consequences of which you can't control. This book isn't about race relations, so I'll speak from a male perspective about the downside of being a woman. I know every woman knows what it's like more than I do, but I'm speaking because I *was* a part of the side causing the pain. I'd like to explain what it is and why it is.

Men operate from fear. Fear is the reason men join gangs. Fear is the reason men join fraternities. Fear is the reason men get tattoos. Fear is the reason men do anything, really. Some men come into this knowledge and consciously change the place from which they operate. Men join gangs out of fear of being bullied or fear of being seen as uncool. Men get tattoos out of fear of being seen as soft, uncool, or unattractive to women. Men join fraternities out of fear of being left out, ostracized, seen as uncool or unconnected. Yes, there are real reasons and positive reasons why we do some of these things, too, but if you dig deep enough, the root is fear—not love. Fear is the same reason a man will deny this truth to himself and to his woman reading this book. A man will say, "That's just Tony's opinion; he's only speaking for himself." I am speaking from experience, but some truths are universal. If you get to the root of things, what sense does it make to do a lot of what we do?

I decided to rush for a fraternity in college. I did it because my teammate asked me to do it. He did it because his father and his brother were a part of the same fraternity. As I started the process, I noticed a void in every man I met. They were either challenged in their looks, socially awkward, or unique in their own way or had been starved of male attention or companionship. The big brother told me he had joined the fraternity because he had grown up with three sisters and a single mother. Others told me they had joined for the connections after college. As I went through the process, it wasn't adding up. They were telling me they were breaking me down to then build me up. So they slapped me on my bare chest, yelled in my face, ran me over running full speed in a muddy field—for what? To join a group of guys I didn't like, pay dues to something I didn't understand, just to wear letters and be a part of the group at parties? I dropped out. The guys I met were operating from fear and/or insecurity. What other reason is there to pay to be beat on and cursed out? I see a lot of those guys from fraternities asking me for help today. Why do you need my connections or me as a connection? I thought that was what the group was for—or was it? Is it really that you wanted to be seen as cool and attractive to the college women? Let's be honest here. Men hate this kind of talk. This talk is confrontational. It's seen as disrespectful. We get so lost in the sauce that the truth is a disease. We don't evaluate why we do what we do.

I got tattoos in college to look sexy to women and tough to guys. Let's be honest: if you have tattoos, even one of them is for a loved one you lost. You didn't need a tattoo for that, though. You just decided to make it mean something since you were getting it anyway. What's the real reason you got it? Because you saw another man with it? Because the thugs or the cool guys you saw growing up had them? Because the markings of tattoos would detour the bullies? What is the real reason? No, dig deeper. The first thought you had when you decided to get a tattoo was what? Only you know the real truth. Did you want to be cool? Did you want to stand out? Did you want to fit in? Or do you just love a painful needle poking your skin to leave permanent ink on it? Do you just love art? Do you love body art because of the beauty and historical meanings behind it? If a man can be honest with himself about why he does the things he does, our world can change for the better.

Men operate from fear, pain, and insecurity more often than any other feelings. I remember when my son was really little and we went to a resort in Cancún. We were about to go to the pool. My son asked me if I had to take my shirt off. I told him yes. He asked me because he didn't like the tattoos on my chest and stomach and wanted to know if I'd keep my shirt on to conceal them. Tattoos make no sense to the mind of a child. In that moment, I realized they made no sense to me, either. What logical sense does it make to permanently mark your body based on a temporary thought or feeling? How will you look at eighty years old with a body full of tattoos? I ask men these questions to start the process of doing the work. We have to do the real work—the inner work. If we are afraid to confront ourselves, we can't move forward in a positive and productive manner.

Confrontation of self leads to discovery and inner truth. That truth is a divine truth that will unlock the secrets of life and manifest every righteous desire of your heart. At our core, we want peace and prosperity. It's impossible to have those things if you're lying to yourself. Only you can discover your inner truth. I can lead you to the water, but I can't make you drink. I can give you the knowledge, but I can't make you think. You have to confront yourself. You live with the fruit. But have you analyzed your root? If we sat down in conversation and I posed these questions, trying to point you to your inner truth, it might lead to a fistfight. I'd have to defend myself against the male ego. I've had these conversations with men in person, and they would start yelling and screaming at me, trying to scare me to stop asking life-altering questions. I once had a similar conversation with a guy who weighed over three hundred pounds, and one blow from him in the right place could have taken my life. As I questioned him and dug deeper, he began to yell at me, but at the same time, he was crying. My heart skipped a beat when he yelled at me. I felt his anger. He'd never been that deep. To this day, he still hasn't confronted his inner truth. The truth is too real for most of us. It requires change, and change is painful.

I remember asking a pro athlete who earns over $20 million a year about the trend of tattoos in his sport. He'd answered every other question I had asked, but the tattoo question never received an answer. I searched pictures of pro athletes from their rookie years and then pictures from their fourth or fifth years. In a lot of men, there is a drastic change. I can't call it growing up or maturing, because the pictures suggest otherwise. I noticed a trend of fitting in, insecurity, and ego. I've heard the term "fragile male ego," and I realize now that I'm not sure if I've ever seen an ego that isn't fragile. We confuse arrogance with confidence because of our insecurity. We call ourselves the greatest because no one else is calling us that. We boast and brag about our accomplishments because they define us. Confidence is quiet. Insecurity is loud and speaks even when not asked to. To confront our insecurity is so painful, we don't even venture near it. Anyone who tries to help us uncover our truth is in imminent danger. We guard our inner truth like a vicious dog guarding its master. Your inner truth should be your master, but instead, we mask it with insecurity and lies to ourselves.

It's a man's world because we've forced the issue. On average, men are physically stronger than women. We've equated that strength with leadership. The strongest person isn't always the smartest or the wisest. Muscles have nothing to do with the brain. We've ignored that fact for centuries. The fact that women live longer than men, give birth to children, and think with both sides of the brain has been swept under the rug. It's a painful truth for men to realize that God showed favor when designing a woman. Yes, women have some unfortunate things their bodies go through that no man would trade places to experience. As men, we truthfully have it very easy. I say it to myself all the time—I couldn't imagine bleeding for a week and going about my life as if nothing is happening. What is menopause? I couldn't begin to tell you. Giving birth? I've read that giving birth is equivalent to breaking twenty bones at the same time. The thought of that nearly sends me into shock. As a man, I had to be real with myself. After I broke many hearts and took many women for granted, my wife brought me to my knees in the realization that she is not less than I. Truthfully, she is not my equal. She is greater. I have no desire to pander to women. If this were the days of old, men would stone me to death and laugh with every throw just for mentioning these things. Someone who looks like me and who has walked the path I've walked has to tell the unadulterated truth: This should not be a man's world.

We look at the world at large, but we don't break the world down to what it really is. The world is made up of a bunch of people who are divided by individual families, birthed by women and nurtured by women. Very few men have decoded the matrix and become the one a child runs to when he or she is sick or hurt. In most cases, it's Mom. I've learned in the cases when my sons come to me hurting or sick, it's because their mom isn't home or because they are trying to milk their sickness to get new toy from Daddy. When you look at pro athletes and men who have made a lot of money, how many of them brag about what they've done for their dad? Everyone wants to buy their mom a house and a car. Everyone wants to retire their mom. My dad was in my life every step of the way, but when I made it, I retired my mom, not my dad. I bought my mom a new car, not my dad. I give my mom money each month, not my dad. I love my dad with all of me, but for some reason, I see a man differently than I see a woman, even though he was there for me and still is here for me.

My point is that women are problem solvers. Women are nurturers. Women are managers. Women are the brains of the operation. In most marriages, men say, "I have to ask my wife, and I'll get back to you." You've also heard the phrase "Happy wife, happy life." Well, why don't we say, "Happy women, happy country"? Why have we debased the woman and made her the footstool of society? Why did we have forty-plus presidents before a woman even had a chance at winning? What's the difference between running a home and running the country? If a man can't run a home, how can he run a country? Yes, this realization hurts for me as well as every other man, but I've come to realize that it's simple logic we've overlooked for centuries. Why? Because of fear. Men operate from fear. Fear is the cause of slavery. Fear is the cause of racism. Fear is the cause of bigotry. Fear is the cause of sexism. Fear is the cause of misogyny.

Mi-sog-y-ny (noun): Dislike of, contempt for, or ingrained prejudice against women.

Why does the word *misogyny* exist? How can contempt for women be ingrained? Why would a man dislike, feel contempt for, or have an ingrained prejudice against women? It's all because of fear. We fear what we don't understand. I dislike animals because I don't understand them. They can't speak, so I don't know what they are thinking or what they need, so I fear them. I fear that their innate defense mechanisms are stronger and more dangerous than mine. I fear that in a fight with an animal, I'll lose. I realize that the same way I see animals is the same way a racist person sees me. He fears me because he doesn't understand me, and that fear leads to hate. He feels that in a fight with me, he will lose. He feels that in a battle with me, I will overtake him and take everything he owns. So his defense mechanism is to hate me. That same type of fear is what creates misogyny. At the core of a man, we know that most women are better rounded than us. We also know that a woman can do just about anything we can do. If she can't do it physically, she can create a way to get it done. We fear that in a battle with a woman, we will lose. Therefore, we use the system at hand to suppress women into a role of unhealthy submission in the home and in the workplace. This is all too real. It's a truth we don't want to admit because we fear losing control and the social norms to which we've become accustomed.

On Instagram, I occasionally do a Q and A. Once a woman asked, "If I don't cook and clean for my boyfriend, how can I show him I'm wife material?" That question stopped me in my tracks. The question floored me and taught me so much. The question implies that wives are there to cook and clean, and if a woman doesn't do so, she's not a wife. She has an entire brain that functions on a level unknown to mankind because she's been reduced to cooking and cleaning. Ironically, many of the world-renowned chefs are men, but it's women we've made the cooks in the home. Where did we go wrong?

I realized that when I made my world my wife's world as well, things got better. Some of my greatest strides have come from her suggestions. She magnifies or multiplies everything I bring to her. A man gives a woman sperm, and look what her body creates from it. A woman gets a house and makes it a home. How can women manage every moving part of what makes up the country but not be chosen to run the country? How can women be included in every important decision a man makes and the rearing of the world's greatest humans but not be given full credit for the contributions to society? We have Black History Month because an entire race suffered in America. I don't know of a women's month. International Women's Day is on my birthday, March 8. Maybe that's why God chose me to help lead this movement. I don't think it strange or a coincidence that my life has brought me to this point of realization or recognition. Women can fight for women, but until men fight for women, we haven't grown as a people.

I think it's time we start to get to the root as men. Identify where you're operating from and why. Be very truthful with yourself about why you may cheat on a woman. What was the reason you tried to control a woman? Then identify how what we do in our relationships shapes the world. From the White House to your house. Is it a man's place to run everything and have the final say in what is and isn't done? Do you truly value the mind of your woman? Yes, you may have an order in your home that says you are the head, but does your woman have a voice? Even if society as a whole operates as if it's a man's world, we can start in our own homes to find balance and synergy in our voices and efforts. I believe a woman was placed on Earth to make everything she touches greater. I've experienced this in my marriage. By no means am I saying that women are perfect. I'm saying that even their imperfections may have something to do with the way we as men treat them. If you give a woman a good father and/or a good husband, or if a woman has no man in her life but isn't harassed or abused by men, she will produce on a level unimaginable. As men, we've altered the course of women and our world by operating from fear instead of from love.

Sheri's Perspective

I grew up with a very strong Jamaican mom, so I never had the image that this is a man's world and we as women just live in it. I didn't realize that was a real narrative until I got older and discovered that many women feel as if they are made to be subservient to men. There is a big difference between being submissive and subservient, and I now realize that a lot of people confuse the two.

I was never taught that the only goal I was supposed to have was to grow up and get married to be a wife. I was an athlete growing up, so I spent a lot of late nights at games. I was never taught to cook dinner every night or take care of the household. I am not saying those aren't great things to know, but because I wasn't raised with those things at the forefront of my mind, I never viewed male-female roles the same way as other people did. I saw my single mom be who she was and do what she needed to get stuff done. And I saw her do the same when she was married. Watching her, I realized that people could be the same with or without a relationship. She never once complained about being lonely when she wasn't in a relationship. I also watched her walk away from a marriage that had become toxic, without missing a beat. Seeing that, I never thought of dating as a priority when other girls were obsessed with it. I realized that marriage is great but my happiness would not be determined by what relationship I was or wasn't in. My goals were about my future, getting a full scholarship to school, and becoming a doctor; everything else was just extra.

When I did begin to date, I valued myself and what I wanted for myself so much that I didn't even consider being with someone if it didn't make me happy. At the time I didn't realize how important it was, but I understand its power now. As a woman in this so-called man's world, we have so much more power than we could ever imagine. That power is in the form of influence. But that influence can be unlocked only when you learn to love yourself and value yourself. With those things in your arsenal you can literally change the world—well, at least *your* world. The influence you have can change how everyone around you operates and can leave a lasting impression on every relationship you enter into.

KEY TAKEAWAYS

+ You can be submissive without being subservient.
+ Your power is in the form of influence.
+ True influence is unlocked when you love yourself and understand your worth.

Chapter 2

KNOW YOUR WORTH

I know it sounds simple, but it may be the furthest thing from simple. Who truly knows their own worth? I'm not even sure I know mine. It's actually easier to see the worth in others than in yourself. I can easily see the worth of a woman, even when I struggle to see my own. For many years, I didn't know the worth of a woman because most of the women I met didn't know, either. It wasn't until I met my wife that I truly learned the worth of a woman. I unofficially became a relationship coach in the tenth grade, when I started taking three-way calls from female friends to answer their questions about guys. I became a professional relationship coach at the age of twenty-three. I know that sounds young, but it's because even at twenty-three, I understood more about men than women twice my age did. That was possible because men don't reveal much about themselves in the game of love. When I started telling the secrets of my own mind, many women realized that I wasn't too different from the men in their lives. I say that there are two types of men in the world: grown men and grown boys.

In the dirty games men play, it's important to note that the women who are being taken advantage of don't know their worth. A man who is out to take advantage of you will point out all your flaws and short-comings to minimize your worth in your own mind. He is human and knows how humans work. You'll be reminded of how many men you've slept with, how many kids you've had, how much education you lack, and every flaw you have on your face and on your body. All of those are attempts to devalue you and make you feel less than so you will give more of yourself to him. It's not exclusive to relation-ships. It happens in every arena of life. People ask me where I received my training and what qualifies me to do what I do, as if a man can truly qualify another human. Qualification comes from God—not man. The same goes for women. You're worthy because you are fear-fully and wonderfully made, not because you fit inside a man's box of beauty.

Everyone knows your worth, but no one will tell you unless you know. If you don't know your worth, no one will tell you what you're worth. By not telling you what you're worth to them, you are cheap-ened and you accept less than you deserve. Sometimes you have to let a person think you don't know your worth just to see what he'll give you. Then when you see he is trying to get over on you, you sting him with your true value. He'll try to play dumb, and some people will re-fuse to give you what you're worth, no matter how much you demand it. You have to be willing to walk away.

The first thing a man wants is sex. Men want it so badly that we'll do anything to have it. I know it's hard for women to believe, but it's true. If there were a rule that said, "All men must chop off one leg to have sex with a woman," 90 percent of heterosexual men would voluntarily have one leg. It means that much to a man. Most women won't be able to relate because sex may not be that important to them. I wish it were deeper, but it's not. Men go to extreme lengths for that one thing.

You are worth way more than sex, but if you don't understand the power in that, how can you understand the power of your mind? If the number one thing to men means almost nothing to you, where do you put your value? Why give your body away to a man who hasn't worked for your heart and mind? If you value your mind more than your body and you want a man to stimulate your mind, make him work for that first before giving him your body.

The world has worked very hard to make women feel disposable, expendable, and replaceable. The system has worked nearly to perfection on millions of women. I hear the product of this programming when speaking with women. So many women feel like they'll be overlooked or passed over if they don't bend to the sexual demands of a man. Then there are the emotional and spiritual demands that go with them. Before you know it, you will be like a pawn on his chessboard, working to stay in his game. All along, you were the queen on the board—the most powerful piece—and you never knew it. Your mouth may confess that you knew it, but did your actions back it up?

I hear some women say they'd rather have half of a man than no man at all. That's exactly what they end up with: half of a man. We don't always get what we think we're worth, but eventually, we do. If you're willing to hold out, there is a man who is willing to meet you at your worth and not ask you to compromise. I tried to get my wife to compromise time and time again, but she made me do it her way. Anything she did, it was because she wanted to, not because I coerced her. The good and the bad were both her choice. She didn't move at my pace. She moved at hers. To be honest, that's what stopped me in my tracks. I had never dated anyone who didn't do what I wanted, when I wanted. I had always been able to get my way, until I met my wife. That floored me, and I was so intrigued. Every man wants something rare. It doesn't matter if it's cars, jewelry, food, or women; we want something that not everyone else has. When I found a woman who had changed her ways due to her past mistakes and wasn't settling for a man, it pushed me to another level. At first it was a game to me, like a challenge. Then, by the time I got what I wanted, it wasn't a game any longer because working for her heart had made me fall in love with her. I had no desire to take my ball and go home. I wanted to spend the rest of my life with her. She'd won me over by making me work for her heart. A man respects only that which he gains through hard work.

What do you fear? Evaluate your fears, and get to the root of them. Men try to control out of fear. Women give up their control out of fear. Do you fear being alone forever? Do you fear he will leave you if you ask him to wait until marriage for sex? Do you fear he will hurt you physically if you don't agree with him or give him what he wants? If so, that's not the man for you. A relationship shouldn't induce fear. A relationship should establish peace in your life. How can love grow if you're operating from a place of fear every day? That will cause you to do things you regret, and you will become just like the very thing you fear. Your fear of being alone will one day leave you lonely. You will start operating from a place of desperation trying to keep a man. You'll give him what he wants and then realize what he wants still isn't enough to keep him faithful. Then you'll be angry with yourself for not making him hold out for what you wanted, and that will make you resent him. But because you fear being alone, you'll stay with him. You're with him, but you don't really love him. You're addicted to him, and it feels like love. Love brings peace—not anxiety. Love makes you feel whole—not incomplete. You're confusing addiction and love. Addiction brings anxiety, incompleteness, anger, and despair. Just because you're in a relationship and not a drug house, you call it love instead of addiction, but you have it confused.

Know your value, set standards, and don't compromise for anyone. Don't settle for less than you deserve. Almost every man you meet will try to talk you down from your true worth. Men bargain just for the sake of bargaining. If we can get something cheaper than it's worth, we'll take it every time. We may walk away from something just because we can't get it cheaper, even though we know it's worth every dime of the asking price. It's our nature. We take that same thinking into relationships. Most of the time, it's a man's ego that makes him walk away from a woman who won't compromise her values. He knows she's the one and she's worth it, but he hasn't won the battle with his ego yet, so he loses out on the woman of his dreams.

One day, a man will meet a woman and realize that he's passed up on wives in the past and if he continues, he will die lonely. It's not that you're soul mates; it's that you met each other at the right time in life. You're meant for each other because you both have gone through your fair share of heartache and pain. Now you're ready to settle down. He may try to get you to compromise just to see if he can have a footstool for a wife, but if you don't give in, he may ask you to be his wife. If he doesn't, you've lost nothing. You have to rest assured and know that the man for you will work for your heart and wait on you. He will work until you're ready to drop your guard and let him love you.

Imagine going on a job interview and not knowing your worth. You could be worth $100,000 a year but feel worth only $50,000 a year. The interviewer will ask you what you expect to be paid. If you say $50,000, he or she won't say, "No, you're worth $100,000." He or she will say, "Thank you for your suggestion. We'll take that into consideration and let you know if we can meet your demands." The company will make you wait longer than normal to make you sweat and lower your rate even more. It's hoping that in five to seven days, you'll email and say that after some thought, you've decided you can accept $35,000 to start. All along, it had $100,000 budgeted for your position but asked you first just to see if you knew what your position is worth. Think about that. It happens every day. Feel that in your system, and know that's how you've been selling yourself short in your relationships. The company isn't going to give you $100,000 after you've told it you'll accept $35,000. Instead, it's going to hire you and then go out and get two more just like you. Now it has three insecure but hardworking staff for the price of one confident and worthy person. Then, after you've served the company in blood, sweat, and tears, you'll get laid off, only to be replaced by someone who knew her worth.

In a relationship, the same thing happens. You're worth a ring, marriage, and 100 percent commitment. Instead, you accept lip service and inconsistency in exchange for a Facebook status that says "In a relationship." Instead of the man giving you what you're worth, he gets you, drains you, gets two more women just like you, and juggles the three of you. Then, after you've served him with blood, sweat, and tears, he breaks up with you, only for you to see him praising another woman three weeks later, calling her his "rib." A year later, he's walking her down the aisle, calling her the love of his life. You're ready to stab your eyes out with the corner of your cell phone while screaming at God, asking Him why he made you the way you are. You're mad at your ex, mad at God, and somehow still find room to be jealous of the new woman, all because you didn't know your worth. As you question what's wrong with you, you're failing to realize that the other woman met him at the time of her life when she was fed up with the games. She made him level up, and when her saw her full worth, it made him realize his own worth. She made him better by default. You have to accept it for what it is, forgive yourself, learn from it, heal, grow, and move on. Life is to be lived forward—not looking backward. Vow to yourself that you'll never make the same mistake again, and commit yourself to growth and knowledge. Once you know your worth, add tax and interest for the things you've suffered. A man will meet you where you are and love you the way you deserve to be loved. You didn't lose your man; you gave someone else her man to make room for your man. That is the circle of love. It happens to the best of us.

What does your heart need? What are you worth? Are you worth marriage before sex? Are you worth daily communication? Are you worth a date every week? Are you worth meeting his family and friends before being official? You set your standards. Do you want a man who curses and yells at you? Do you want a man who doesn't gamble, smoke, drink, club, or do drugs? Whatever it is you want, you deserve it simply because you say so. It's your birthright. If you're being too picky, life will show you that.

There is a difference between standards and preferences. Standards are rooted in morals and values. Preferences are numbers and things. You may prefer a man who earns $100,000 a year, but that doesn't define a man. You're welcome to wait for that man, but will you be willing to walk away if he doesn't meet your standards? What if he makes $100,000 a year but yells and curses at you? Are you going to compromise your standards to meet your preferences? Understanding your value and what goes into that value is important. It's not just about what you want; it's about what you're worth.

Many women ask, "Can I meet the right man at the wrong time?" My answer is no. If he's the right man, it will be the right time. True love transcends time, and if a man isn't willing to respect your worth, he's not the man for you. Yes, his timing is off because he hasn't grown into the man he's supposed to be, but he's not on your time. He's on someone else's time. When the time is for you, everything will line up. You will know your worth, and he will know how to respect and value a woman's worth. That is when you'll know you're meant for each other. If that's not the case, don't try to stretch a season into a lifetime. Release him.

You should never hold on to someone who doesn't value you. The longer you hold on, the less you become. Desperation sets in, and you will literally lose yourself in the relationship. There are so many women who are going through life feeling worthless and empty, not being able to escape a relationship because they don't feel worthy of pulling themselves up and walking away. Hopelessness starts to set in, and when you settle, you start to sink. It will take an internal wake-up call to give you the boost you need. You have to confront your fears and know that you can start over. There is light at the end of the tunnel, and there is a way out of a toxic relationship. As you confront your fears and refute every lie you're telling yourself, you'll start to find the truth within, and it will strengthen you.

What are you telling yourself? Are you telling yourself that you're not worthy of love? The fear of the unknown holds so many women captive in love with men who don't love them in return. It's always easier said than done, and that's why you have to start doing the talking. Reverse the lies you've been telling yourself, and start speaking life and victory over your situation.

What is the worst that can happen if you walk away? You won't stop breathing, and you won't stop living. There is no sense in going into a marriage if your potential spouse doesn't value you before marriage. Be willing to walk away from the deal. Having the willingness to walk away is what gets you the deal you want and deserve.

After you walk away, men always pretend to respect your worth. The majority of the time, it's his ego talking—not his heart. Pay attention, and you'll know the difference. If you've given a man several years to work with you in a relationship and he still finds a way to make you leave him, it means he's not the one for you. Remember, he already knew your worth; he just chose to ignore it because he wasn't ready, or he didn't give it to you because you didn't know it when you met him.

You can grow into yourself and discover what you deserve years into a relationship, but you can't expect the man to have grown to that point with you. In some cases, that's what will happen, but in others, you grow alone and then you have to leave him because he refuses to respect the new you. I know you want to wait for him to get it right, but you have to consider the fact that every day you live beneath your worth, you're dying a miserable death emotionally and spiritually. You also have to realize that he's had the time to work with you and grow with you, but he chose not to do so. With that in mind, love yourself enough to let go so both of you can grow. You can't force a man to love you, nor can you force a man to respect you. All you can do is stand your ground and be unwilling to accept less than you deserve; he will decide the rest for himself. Accept what he decides, and if he chooses wrong, be woman enough to let him live with his bad decisions. It's the only way he will become a man, and it's the only way you will become a woman.

Know your worth and don't settle for less.

Sheri's Perspective

Many women hear the phrase "Know your worth," but they don't know what that looks like or what it takes to get there. It's not living in a fairy tale or expecting a standard that is unattainable, and it starts before the relationship, not during it. Knowing your worth doesn't mean you are perfect and have no insecurities, because I definitely had my share for sure. It just means you figure out what you will or won't put up with in a relationship and you stick to your guns regardless of what point of the relationship you are in.

I remember when Tony and I had started talking; we weren't officially in a relationship yet, but we were definitely talking a lot and hanging out a lot. One night, a friend of his was hanging out with my apartment mate, and Tony and I were watching a movie in my room. We were lying down, and he kept rubbing his hand up my thigh. I moved his hand a few times, but he kept putting it back. I definitely liked him and thought he was attractive, but I knew I wasn't ready for anything else, so even though it was the middle of the night, I told him he had to go. I remember him being blown away, and he couldn't believe that I was kicking him out of the apartment. In the moment, I didn't really think about the fact that he might never want to talk to me again. I just knew that I felt uncomfortable with the situation. I didn't want things to escalate further at that point, so I did what came natural to me, and that was to remove myself from the situation. Knowing your worth can look like that and can be as simple as removing yourself from a situation that makes you feel uncomfortable. I knew there was no way someone I wasn't even officially dating was going to have those privileges, so I stopped things as soon as I felt they were starting to get out of hand. If I hadn't thought about the standards that mattered to me before that encounter, it would've been much harder to respond in that way.

I remember another time early on during our relationship; we had gotten into an argument. Tony started raising his voice and yelling. Immediately, I told him, "Don't yell or raise your voice at me!" I walked away from him, grabbed my keys, and left our apartment early to go to work. I didn't answer the phone the rest of the day; it gave me time to cool down and him as well. That's another example of what knowing your worth can look like. I had seen enough toxic relationships growing up to know I wanted no part of one for myself. I knew that if I let yelling be okay, then grabbing would be okay, next would be pushing, and so on and so forth. When he raised his voice at me and started yelling at me, it made me feel uncomfortable, so I removed myself from the situation. In that moment, it helped him see what was important to me and what I wouldn't tolerate. I don't want you to think I'm this superstrong person who can just walk away from any situation and not feel anything; that's definitely not the case. It is okay to show a tough face and then cry when you get in the car. It is okay to hide your phone because you don't have the willpower not to answer it. Those things are okay; just because you know your worth doesn't mean it's always easy to stick to your principles. When you have feelings for someone, things always get harder; don't be under the impression I was able to do this without any sadness or vulnerability, because that's definitely not the case. You just have to prioritize yourself and be okay with those feelings, regardless of what the outcome may be.

When you think about the standards that matter to you, really think about them. Don't make up things just to look like you respect yourself with the thought that it'll make someone marry you. Some men will leave and never look back, and you have to be okay with that. If you know your worth and the standards you set mean something to you, the right person will respect them and respect you because of it. Keep in mind that it may take walking away from quite a few wrong ones before you find the right one.

KEY TAKEAWAYS

✦ Know your worth, set standards, and refuse to compromise.

✦ Don't be afraid to stand up for what you feel is right.

Chapter 3

POWER VERSUS INFLUENCE

I was traveling the world speaking on love and relationships, and at one of my seminars, a lady said to me, "Men have power; women have influence." That stuck with me. I was teaching that women have all the power, but when the lady said that to me, it shifted my mind-set and I understood exactly what she meant from that day on. We've seen men as presidents and CEOs, but we never take into consideration that there's a woman coaching them during pillow talk sessions.

There are countless prostitutes and escorts around the world who are responsible for some of the largest business deals to ever take place, and they'll never get the credit for it. Those very women who chose that line of work as their best option could just as easily have become CEOs. For whatever reason, that's how life works sometimes. I've seen in movies where a man hires a woman for a night of pleasure, and then, the next morning, he's running business ideas by her as she's smoking her morning cigarette. The woman calmly and succinctly answers the man with a piercing confidence and assurance that send shock waves up his spine. He looks at her in awe and realizes that if the circumstances had been different, she could have been his wife. I personally know women who went from stripping on a pole to owning businesses and earning millions of dollars each year—from broken to blessed. There are housewives and working wives around the world supporting men who are leading companies. The man stands in front of the boardroom sounding like a genius. No one in the room knows that the night before, his wife developed the entire plan he is pitching. He's praised as a genius and visionary, but truthfully, he's the beneficiary of a woman's wisdom at work.

I can attest to the validity of the claims I'm making. I've amassed more than three million supporters online, spoken on three different continents, worked with celebrities and corporations as a life coach, and the list goes on. All of the success I've had to date has been a result of my wife's influence in my life. I kid you not. Yes, God blesses me. Yes, I have received divine favor from God. But my change was inspired by my wife.

I've written entire books based on one suggestion from my wife. I've created campaigns and developed new offers for my followers based on an idea from my wife. She doesn't do what I do, and she has no desire to. In the midst of her hectic schedule, she takes the time to speak into my life, help me find clarity, and influence me to take action. Her influence has also saved my butt time and again. I would have filed for bankruptcy three or four times by now had I acted on some of my ideas; having her to talk me out of them has been my saving grace. I'd never considered the role of a woman beyond sex and raising kids when I was under the programming of society. I still don't think the world at large understands the gifts we are suppressing in women today. I titled this book and I'm doing the bulk of the writing, but the idea to stay in this lane was my wife's. I was tired of talking about love and relationships. It was so hard breaking the "guy code" over and over again. Life became lonely after losing all my male friends because of my message. There isn't a man who knows me who hasn't had his toes crunched by the messages I share online. Guys treat me like the plague unless they need something from me. I was ready to throw in the towel, and I did for a bit. I started teaching about business and entrepreneurship. I felt better about it. I was in a different lane—a comfortable space. Then something happened. My reach online went way down. As a result, my income went way down. At first I didn't understand the correlation, but then I went to my wife in a moment of frustration and she spoke into my life. She told me that I was out of alignment with my purpose. She helped me see how I had become interested in business and entrepreneurship because that was the stage of life I was in, but it wasn't really my calling to teach about it. Then she made a lot of references to other speakers who speak on business and how their lives are probably a mess behind closed doors. There was also a clear difference in our income. Those guys earned millions of dollars a year, and some earned millions of dollars a month. They were qualified to teach on business. I wasn't. My wife helped me understand that what they've done in business is equivalent to what I've done in relationships. I'd had way more experience with women than any of those guys, so my understanding of the dynamics of relationships is like none other. As she laid it out to me, it started to make sense. I didn't want to hear it because walking in purpose can be so painful at times, but God rewards those who are faithful. My wife showed me the guys who had seen my blueprint as a love and relationship teacher and decided to follow in my footsteps. It was clear that there's a need for these lessons, and she told me that if I don't do it, God will send someone who will. She pointed out the difference between me and some others who she could tell weren't living the life I'm living behind the scenes and how they were in it only for the money. As a woman using her intuition, she could tell the real from the fake. She pointed out the fake but also showed me how the world ate it up like it was real. Then she helped me understand how the system of supply and demand works and how I would be replaced and lose my seat at the table, even though I'm one truly called by God. Her message floored me. It was real. It hurt. I didn't want to hear it, but I listened. I assumed my position at the table and reluctantly started to walk in my purpose again. The by-product of obedience was rewards I didn't request—things like speaking engagements, book sales, course sales, and so on. It was like God patting me on the back and saying "Good job, son." Our income went up by 400 to 700 percent some months. My success is determined by my obedience to my calling. I still struggle with it today because there are so many fakes that it makes me feel fake when I'm walking in my calling. My wife told me that it doesn't matter how many fakes there are; the people want the real and they will recognize the real when they see it. God used my wife to speak into my life and to get me back on course. I don't think anyone else could have reached me the way she did. That's when I started to understand a woman's influence. I get the credit for what I create, but a lot of it comes from her influence in my life. She told me not to worry about money and how I would earn it. Even in the beginning of our journey, when we had only $25 a month left after paying our bills and had to live on that for two weeks until the next paycheck, she kept a smile on her face and told me to stay the course and not veer off. I tried to get off, and she would get me back on. My wife told me that money doesn't matter to her; love does. As long as I was ambitious, consistent, and obedient to the Will of God, she'd be in my corner.

As I began to study the text of the Holy Bible, I started in the beginning. Though I'd read the story of Adam and Eve a million times, I'd never considered the underlying message. I'd always thought the message was that man has a sinful nature and the reason we are in the mess we are in today is that the first two humans decided to sin against God. Many have said the story is fictional and is just a metaphor for life. But I was captivated and read it as my truth. As I looked back on the story from a different perspective, I got a different message from it. Now the message to me is about a woman's influence. Adam was given the entire world. He was tasked with the job of naming every animal, and he was made in God's image. He was the man. Adam was put in charge over everything, and then woman was made. Eve wasn't given the same rights and privileges as Adam. Her sole purpose was to be a helper to Adam. It was as if she had been created only to assist Adam in the work he was called to do. Then the shift happened. Adam was put in charge, but Eve influenced him to sin against his Maker. Eve's words became more powerful to Adam than the words of God. God told Adam what to do, and Eve told him something else to do. Adam chose his rib over his creator. God knew what He'd set in motion, and free will was granted. But is a man's will really free? Or is a man's will only that which a woman allows it to be?

A woman is the most influential being on the face of the earth. With a simple suggestion, Eve turned the world upside down and introduced sin to all mankind. The Devil knew who had the power. He approached Eve purposely because he knew that a woman thinking with both sides of her brain would be her undoing. He could reason with woman, but Adam was too simpleminded to understand the power of what the Devil would have asked him to do. Adam was a soldier for God and the only person who could make him go against his orders from God was Eve. Whether you believe the story is literal or not, it represents something very powerful. It says to me that a woman can change the world with her influence. If she uses her influence for good, she can change the world for good. If she uses her influence for evil, she can change the world for evil. It all depends on who is speaking to her and who she decides to listen to. If you want, you can blame Eve for the state of our world today. On the other side of that notion, you can see the bigger picture, and that is the influence of a woman.

I continued to study this influence, and I read the story of Samson and Delilah. God had given Samson uncommon strength and no *man* could defeat Samson. That's because they used their physical strength against him. Then along came Delilah. She got close to him, and he fell in love with her. She was bribed to get Samson to reveal the source of his strength to her. She tried and tried and failed. Then, after she convinced Samson that he didn't trust her, he wanted to prove his trust. In proving his trust, he told her that his strength lay in his hair. As he was sleeping, she instructed someone to cut his hair, and then she was able to turn him over to those who had bribed her. No man could have gotten Samson to tell his secret. It was a woman who was used by the adversary to deceive Samson. As you unpack the story, you can walk away with a lot of messages. We can see the negative and call women evil and conniving, or we can consider the circumstances and recognize the strength in a woman's influence.

I decided to take a holistic approach and seek to understand how my role in Sheri's life influenced her to influence me in a positive way. I read in Ephesians 5 to love my wife as Christ loves the church. I accept responsibility for my actions and then move forward with a new love for my woman. In return, she pushes me into greatness because she is operating from a place of love due to my love for her. I also realize my power in every situation and understand that even if a woman's influence is negative, I have the power to deny it if I please. It all works together. Some women use their influence for negative purposes because of the hurt and pain they've experienced. Some women use their influence from a place of ignorance. Even if a woman doesn't understand the power of her influence, the influence is still there. How a woman uses her influence can alter the world she lives in. The way a woman influences her children will be either her crowning glory or her robe of shame. The way a woman influences her man will directly affect her life in the long run. She will either help create a grown boy or help create a grown man. A woman's influence will be either her saving grace or her destruction.

Overall, studying the Bible showed me that women are influential even when not given a position of power. It also showed me that women are not perfect and should not be revered as such. Women are humans who can be flawed, just like men. But a woman's influence is second to none. I believe that a man has the power to love a woman into positive influence, which in turn will only make his life better.

The lesson I took away from my study of the Bible is that no woman should be taken for granted. A man's sin catches up to him, and eventually he meets his match. For every good man, there is a good woman who can make him great. For every evil man, there is a scorned woman who can end his life of misery with an untimely death. I mean what I said. A man playing with the hearts of women will meet his demise, whether literally or figuratively. A woman is not to be played with like a game. Some women will suffer and endure mistreatment at the hands of a man, and others will fight back in a way that destroys a man from the inside out.

Every woman on Earth has a level of influence that even she may not understand. I believe the axiom that behind every good man there is a great woman. Women become therapists, life coaches, doctors, counselors, prophets, teachers, friends, and much more to the people in their lives. Even women who have been abased are powerful beyond measure. No woman is insignificant, whether she be your mother, sister, wife, girlfriend, aunt, cousin, friend, or daughter. Men, please understand that you are being influenced and it is for the good of your life, or for the bad. You have to identify which it is and not be fooled by your own strength and wisdom. Don't let your power produce conceit in your heart. In an instant, you can be ruined by the influence of a woman. On the other hand, if you respect God's creation, your life can be changed for the better just as quickly as it can be ruined.

I recently read the book of Esther in the Bible, and it floored me. Esther was chosen to be one of the queens to King Xerxes of Persia. In those days, the queen really was powerless in many ways. She could approach the king only *if he requested* her presence. She didn't live with him and sleep in bed with him every night. She had to stay in the queen's quarters. Xerxes had many concubines and slept with a different woman every night if he wanted to. Then the woman had to return to her room, where she would continue to be pampered and taken care of until the king requested her presence again. Today, this is the same as what men refer to as a side chick or jump-off. How can a woman in this role have any influence in a man's life? After he met Esther, Xerxes was enthralled by her beauty and presence. And so Esther was able to approach the king and break the law of the land without being killed. She did what she wanted to do, and the king was so wrapped up in her presence that he allowed it. There was a man in the kingdom named Haman who hated the Jews. Esther used her position to get next to the king, and she asked him if she could prepare a banquet for him and Haman. The king agreed, and they showed up for dinner. At the dinner, Esther told Xerxes that she was actually a Jew and that his dear buddy next to him, Haman, had a plan to kill all the Jews. The king was enraged and ordered Haman to be executed. Just because of Esther's position in the king's life. Xerxes went against everything he had already agreed to, broke several traditions, and ordered his chief-in-command to be murdered, all because of the request of Esther.

I've suffered at the hands of a woman's influence, and I've succeeded at the hands of a woman's influence. I believe every man has, but because we've been conditioned to see the woman as a weaker vessel and nearly powerless, we don't give her credit for what she can do. I've heard women's stories of luring men with sex, drugging them, and robbing them of all their possessions. I've heard stories of women, even in modern days, who have set men up to be killed. At the same time, women have set men up to live, to be promoted, exalted, and successful beyond their wildest dreams. When will we realize and respect the influence of women and channel it in a healthy and positive way for the benefit of mankind? I hope this book gets into the right hands and begins a shift in our world that appreciates, respects, and values the hearts and minds of our women so that we can win as people. We are teammates—not opponents. We have to stop trying to defeat our women and start trying to uplift them, so in return, they can use their gifts to make the world a better place.

If you're a woman reading this, please recognize what you possess. If you're a man reading this, please respect what your woman possesses.

Sheri's Perspective

In-flu-ence (noun): The capacity to have an effect on the character development, or behaviour of someone or something, or the effect itself.

Influence is a huge thing to have, and it can change someone's life drastically in a positive or negative way, based on how you use it. Until I listened to one of Tony's messages years ago, I didn't really understand the influence I had in his life. But it was amazing to learn how our late-night conversations really resonated with him and made a difference in how he handled future decisions.

Influence is about speaking life into someone and being able to lift him up or inspire him in times of weakness, with your words. Before you can have anything meaningful to say, you have to first listen and be interested in someone's ups, downs, and everything in between. That means being an active listener in his conversations about their passions, work, etc., even when you're exhausted after a long day. Your heart also has to be in the right place; you have to speak from a place of love. It's not about your own selfish wants or desires. And last but most important, you have to be in prayer. God can't speak through you if you are never receiving from Him.

For Tony and me, these opportunities almost always occur late at night, after the kids are asleep and we are lying in bed just talking. He may express frustrations, pose a question, or just want to talk about an idea. I first listen to what he is talking about thoroughly, ask questions if I don't totally get it, and then look at the big picture before I give an opinion. And even if I disagree with the idea or have a difference in opinion, I make sure to express it in love. I explain why I feel that way and what I think he should do differently. Almost every night when we get our kids into bed, I am exhausted, and my eyes start closing before my head hits the pillow. But I know these talks are important and necessary, so I will always stay up when he has something to talk about. Sometimes we will talk for hours and hours, even when I know my 5:00 a.m. wake-up call is fast approaching. Every person needs someone to talk to who has his or her best interests at heart. When you can be that person for your significant other, it makes a world of difference.

KEY TAKEAWAYS

✦ Influence is the capacity to have an effect on a person (positively or negatively).

✦ Be an active listener in day-to-day conversations and show you care.

✦ Speak from a place of love; even disagreement should be said in a way of love. Never condescend or ridicule an idea or a plan.

✦ Make time to be your partner's confidant when he or she needs you the most.

✦ Stay in prayer so God can speak through you with just the right words for the situation.

Chapter 4

THE GROWN-BOY SYNDROME

Of course this is a term I made up, but it describes the behavior I see from men most often. In my humble opinion, every man is a grown boy until he meets the right woman. Many men disagree with me on that, but meeting the right woman and treating her the way God intended for her to be treated matures a man in a way like nothing else. It's a rite of passage for a man. There is something about selflessness and love that helps a man reach places he's never been before. In the depths of a man's heart are reservoirs of love waiting to be tapped into. Most men never utilize that love supply and die without having ever really lived. I'm committed to helping men reach a new level of living through loving.

A grown boy is an adult male who has passed the age of eighteen in years but isn't mature. If a man refuses to grow, he actually starts to go backward. There are fifteen-year-old boys who treat women better than some forty-year-old men do. In fact, a man's heart is purer at fifteen than it is at forty. At forty, a man's heart can be scarred and callused from years of toxic relationships. If a man goes through a series of rejections and disappointments, he can grow bitter and resentful toward women. With every passing year, he becomes a worse human being if thing aren't going his way in the love department. It's painful being a man who hasn't surrendered to love. Both men and women were created to love, but men who reject love and healthy relationships suffer in silence until the effects of that suffering start to show publicly. Maybe you've seen it before, but you probably didn't know or understand the underlying causes of the man's behavior. A man without real love—even for self—becomes nearly unbearable. Love is the greatest gift given to mankind, and you can't create a meaningful life if you don't evolve into your highest self through love.

You may not want to hear this next statement, but I have to share it anyway. Most men are looking for a mother they can sleep with. Sounds like incest, right? Well, I don't mean it in that sense, but it's very close. Men are babied and catered to by women from the time we come out of our mother's womb. Many a single mother makes her son her husband. She caters to his every need, and because she doesn't have a man in her life, she treats her son like her man. She cuddles with him, kisses him, buys him everything he asks for, dresses him like she'd want her man to dress, and the list goes on. The young boy then forms an emotional relationship with his mother that is very strong. He depends on her for everything. She is his life coach, his confidante, his bail bondsman, his chef, his maid, his chauffer, his stylist, his assistant, his CEO, and much more. Women are nurturers by nature. Therefore, if a woman doesn't have a husband to take care of, she gravitates to the next closest option, and that's her son. It's not intentional; it's instinctual. She's fulfilling her purpose by loving and caring.

When God created woman, He said, she will come from man and she will be a *helpmeet*—a helper—to him. God knew men needed women, and he created it as such. A man can do everything for himself, but nothing feels quite like a woman doing it for you. It's both mental and emotional. There is a high a man gets when a woman serves him in any way. "Acts of service" is a love language, according to Dr. Gary Chapman, the author of *The 5 Love Languages*, and most men love that one to be spoken frequently. You will notice it in little boys as well as in grown men. I'm raising two sons with my wife. I see them ask their mother to do the simplest things, like cut up their food, open the ketchup packet, squirt the ketchup. My wife, being a lover and nurturer, races over to do it. Up to a certain age, it's necessary. Then there comes a time when children must learn how to do for themselves, especially young boys—because the nature of a man says they will allow others to do things for them. When my boys were around five years old, I started to step in and teach them things from a man's perspective. My son would ask his mother to open the ketchup packet. I'd stop her as she'd race over, I'd grab the packet, and then I'd give my son a tutorial on how to open the packet and spread the ketchup on his fries. He'd listen to me and then try it again. His eyes would light up as if he'd discovered the treasure at the end of the rainbow. *There you go, son—now you're a man.*

Little by little, I teach my sons how to be men and to do for themselves. My wife does the same and is starting to teach them how to cook, clean, do laundry, and so on, so they won't have to depend on a woman. I've had to step in and cut her off sometimes, because as a mother, she's willing to do the work instead of letting them do certain things for themselves. Of course, she'd stop at some point, but I like to push the limits and get our boys started earlier than we might think is possible. If I'm wrong, I get out of the way and let my wife continue to do as she was doing. But I have to try because I'm a man, and I understand how boys can become grown boys if we aren't taught properly while growing up.

We have more single moms today than ever before. There was a time when divorce and sex before marriage, or having a child out of wedlock, were a cardinal sin. Now to have a child out of wedlock is almost the standard. So is divorce. It's very normal, and we don't frown at it as much. We are living in a no-judgment zone, so even accountability is seen as judgment, and no one wants to be held accountable. So what does that produce? Grown boys. Grown boys are men who want pleasure without pain. The pain is the pain of discipline and responsibility. They're painful because they require sacrifice and commitment. That's too much to ask of a lot of men today. Men today want to have sex and do everything it takes to create a baby, but then they walk out on the responsibility of raising the child. A man gets a woman pregnant and then hates the woman for having a baby. "You have the audacity to have a body that creates babies?" demands the grown boy. "Are you kidding me? How dare you allow your body to reproduce a human for whom I'll be responsible for the next eighteen years?"

This behavior is showing up in many ways. In a microwave society, people want microwave success. People want money-producing trees. Life is a party. Live it up. Men play video games all week, while their child does backstrokes in the bathtub for an hour. Clubbing on the weekends. Forty is the new twenty. No, forty is still forty, and it's time to act like you're forty. Grown boys feel judged, disrespected, and unappreciated. I was that man, but I had to be called out to make some changes in my life. There was a day when holding your neighbor accountable was expected and respected. Today, accountability is a curse word. We have to face the music and do what we can to change it.

A man who is raised by a woman who oversteps her boundaries as a mother is crippled. He reaches adulthood, and he desires a woman who serves him like his mother did but sleeps with him like he thinks a woman should. When we are trapped in the "grown-boy syndrome," we don't see it as such. We think we are just doing what we're supposed to do. It's normal behavior. In reality, a wife shouldn't be anything like a mom. A mom is supposed to love her son unconditionally. There are conditions to an intimate relationship, like faithfulness, selflessness, respect, loyalty, honesty, trust, and more. A boy can run away from home ten times, and Mom is supposed to let him come back every time. A boy can go to the detention center ten times, and Mom is supposed to let him come home every time. A man can go to jail ten times, and Mom will bail him out every time. Neither a girlfriend nor a wife is supposed to nurture a grown man. Growth, responsibility, and accountability are things a man has to learn on his own through life experience. If he's not learning, growing, and changing, then he's taking life and the woman in his life for granted.

There are grown men and there are grown boys, and you have

to know the difference. A grown man accepts full responsibility for his life. He can do anything and everything for himself, even if his woman does some things for him. If he lies down to make a baby, he stands up to raise it. He doesn't run or hide from responsibility. A grown boy, on the other hand, plays mind games and wants to escape the consequences of his choices. It is not easy for a man to become a grown man, though. Please do not see it as an easy feat that men are skipping over just for the heck of it. Our society reinforces men being lazy and there being a double standard. As men, it's hard for us to admit this. In life itself, being a man is much easier than being a woman is. I'm a man, and I see what my wife goes through every month, and all I can do is rub her back and pray for her. I don't know what it's like to have hormones going crazy and my skin reacting because of it. I've never felt menstrual cramps that hurt so bad they make me want to lie on a cold tile floor or sleep with a heating pad on my stomach. I've never been pregnant. I've never had a period. Growing up, I wasn't an object of lustful men's obsessions, nor was I harassed by women. The life of a man, if we are honest, is easy compared to that of a woman. Naturally, women are more mature than men because life requires them to be more mature. You've heard of men in high places and powerful positions openly admit to sexually harassing women and nothing happened to them. You don't hear that from women in high-ranking positions. Who is paid more in the workplace? I read about an actress who was paid a certain amount for reshoots while her male costar was paid nearly ten times as much. I share this to say that men are raised to be grown boys, and unless we confront this openly, we won't get past it.

Now, all of the men who read this may say I'm being one-sided and it's very hard to be a man, but I'm a man, so I know firsthand what it's like being a man in this world. Even as a black man in the United States, a place known for racism toward blacks, I still can't say life has been terrible. It hasn't been as easy for me as for men from some other races, but it hasn't been hard, either. I can blame racism for my problems if I like, but as a grown man, I choose to accept responsibility for my choices and my destiny instead of blaming the world around me. I believe a man who steps into his fullness can beat the odds and achieve his goals.

I'm hard on grown boys because I was a grown boy myself. I was most likely worse than any man who will read this book. I know that weak love doesn't work to change grown-boy behavior. You need tough love, and you have to be man enough to take it. It's a hard pill to swallow when you realize you've been living beneath your potential. I had to confront some hard truths as I began to make the transition from grown boy to grown man.

For example, is it right to lie to a woman for no reason other than to deceive her and lead her on? Why do we lie to women about small things like how much we earn or how old we are? Sometimes, as men, we lie about the smallest and most insignificant things for no other reason than to practice our lying skills for later use. Is it right to deceive a woman just to get her to like you more or respect you more? As men, we may lie about our income or where we live to make a woman think we are established and financially secure. I know a guy who owned a mansion and his roommate was telling women that the house belonged to him, not the owner. The roommate was living on the bottom floor in a small room that could not be mistaken for the master bedroom, but he was telling women that the house belonged to him and the actual owner of the house was his roommate. What purpose does that serve?

Is it right to cheat on a woman and leave her in the dark as to the games we men play? Why do we let a woman fall in love with us, knowing we barely even like her, only to have her find out we've been cheating on her the entire time, crushing her heart? That is grown-boy behavior. I coach women daily who have given years to a man and sacrificed everything only to find out he has another woman. More than ever before, I'm learning of situations where the man not only cheated multiple times but also impregnated the other woman. Now the woman is forced to make a choice between her love for the man and leaving him, even after all the time and energy she's invested. I was that man in my dating years, and even then it didn't make sense to me.

It's important to understand that every man is a grown boy until he meets the right woman and is ready to become a grown man. Every man has to go through a maturation process, whether in his teens or in his adult years. Some men grow faster than others, and some men never grow. I've seen men who lose woman after woman and still they don't have the heart to become better men. There are men who were raised without love, and that turned them into savage-hearted men who don't know how to love women. A woman has to learn as fast as she can what a grown boy looks like and then lace up her track shoes and run away from him as fast as she can.

Love is love. It doesn't hurt, and it can't be confused. If it hurts, it's not love. If you find yourself settling as a woman and putting up with behavior you don't feel you should be putting up with, you love a grown boy. The longer you stay with him, the more you reinforce his behavior. The more any behavior is reinforced, the more it repeats itself.

Today, women deal with momma's boys more than ever because of how men are being raised by their moms. A man becomes an adult, meets a woman, and then makes his mom and his girlfriend compete for his love. For a grown boy, it's like a sitcom playing out in front of his eyes. He doesn't even need to have a favorite television show because he gets to watch his mom and his girlfriend compete for his love and attention. The woman who is a mother to this adult man may not care enough to speak into her son's life and give him her blessing to meet a woman and ride off into the sunset. But even the Bible encourages it. Genesis 2:24 (KJV) says, "Therefore, a man shall leave his father and his mother, and shall cleave unto his wife; and they shall be one flesh." It's intended for a man to move on from his mom to his wife. But the "grown-boy syndrome" won't allow him to do so. Once you recognize this problem, you have to confront it. Men have to realize when we are being momma's boys, and women have to call it out as well. It's painful to hear for most men, and at first it may cause more problems than it solves, but it's necessary. It's necessary to confront this truth so you can get to the bottom of the issue. A man must find it within himself to grow into the man God intended him to be. That takes accountability and responsibility.

Ladies, stop playing mommy to your grown man. I'm speaking to mothers, girlfriends, and wives. Let him grow. Let him feel the consequences of his choices. Mom, if your grown son gets a woman pregnant, it's not your place to take care of his child while he plays video games or goes to the club. That's not healthy for a man. It hinders his growth. A lot of women have men who are being coddled and babied. A man cheats, lies, steals, and leaves. Then he's allowed to run into and out of your life while you sit still waiting for him to come back and then leave again? You're sitting there stuck like a deer in the headlights, just waiting for his next immature move. You have to recognize the grown-boy behavior and call it out of him. If you speak to it and call it what it is, and let it be known that it won't be tolerated, he will step up in your life and be the man he needs to be, or he will step out of your life so you can heal and grow.

This is the truth of the matter. The truth will hurt before it helps, but let it run its course. You'll come out stronger and wiser.

Sheri's Perspective

Your influence can help you determine whether you are involved with a grown boy or a man. Typically a grown boy likes to take the easy way out, the way of least work or resistance.

Tony and I started our life together really early, and that required a level of maturity we both probably weren't prepared for but had to adjust to immediately. In 2007, I gave birth to our first son, Tony. He was born two and a half months early and spent three and a half months in the neonatal intensive unit. Of course, it was a very stressful and scary time for young parents with no prior experience with something so serious. We were both working for a group home, making decent money, but nothing extravagant. About two months after having our baby, Tony decided he wanted to take the easy way out and go back to the street life, hanging with his boys and making easy money. We had talked about that before, and I had told him that I didn't want him in that life, but of course when times get tough the easy way out seems just that: easy. He couldn't understand at first why I had a problem with it. He said it would bring in more money and that a lot of other women would have been okay with it. I explained to him that I wasn't other women. I didn't care if we were broke or struggling, I didn't want him involved in that life. I told him it was nonnegotiable and if he couldn't be mature and do things the right way, we couldn't be together. I actually ended up leaving for a few days while our baby was still in the neonatal intensive care unit. I think that experience was a wake-up call for Tony; it showed him I was serious, and he decided to step up to the plate. When he realized that living right was more important to me than any amount of money, he respected that and felt less pressure to take the easy way out. He left the grown-boy behavior behind and decided to work hard, make sacrifices, and mature as a man.

Sometimes it takes our being mature and choosing the harder way, the path of most resistance, to evoke change and help our partner transition from a grown boy to a man. It requires a different level of maturity from you as well. You can't expect to have a real man when you are making immature or selfish decisions. Maturity means that even when you are upset or angry, you don't yell or curse but speak in a way that is respectful. Maturity is making financial sacrifices to show your partner that you are a team. Maturity means making sure your relationship with God is where it needs to be through daily devotion and prayer so He can speak through you. Your decisions, your words, and the way you speak life into your partner can positively influence him and help change him from a grown boy to a man.

KEY TAKEAWAYS

+ Don't settle for a grown boy. Your partner should be taking responsibility and making choices that help foster growth.

+ A grown boy plays mind games and doesn't accept responsibity in the relationship. He is constantly making excuses instead of taking action.

+ Influence requires maturity.

+ Be serious, and don't give your man the easy way out; your choices and influence can help change a grown boy to a grown man.

Chapter 5

THE POKER FACE

Have you ever seen a poker tournament on television? They feature the best poker players in the world. I'm sure there has to be a woman in the bunch, but I've never seen her. Google "best poker players in the world." You'll find some pictures of men. You may also find a list of the best current poker players and how much money they made last year. These guys make millions of dollars a year playing poker, a card game. It takes no physical strength to play poker, other than the strength it takes to overcome the stress and anxiety, but a card isn't heavy to lift. Why is it that so many men play poker and so few women do? It's the difference in the mind.

It's important in a relationship to understand the differences between how men and women think. Yes, there are some similarities, but we often behave in vastly different ways. As I watch a poker game, it seems like a game of mostly luck, combined with the skill of knowing how to use the luck you've been dealt. It's also about knowing how to hide your fate so no one else sees you're holding a weak hand. I'm sure it's much deeper if you ask a professional poker player, but a lot of it hinges on emotional intelligence.

In the early stages of life, it's hard to see a difference in the emotional intelligence of boys and girls. Young boys seem to cry just as much as, if not more than, young girls. When I say young, I mean under the age of eight years old. Then a shift happens. Boys start to fight tears and emotions. The world tells us that we can't cry. Because so many men believe that, the rest of us are forced to follow suit. Now there are a bunch of men walking around with a hard shell and a soft inside. The more a man fakes his toughness, the more that muscle is developed. He's developing his emotional intelligence by not giving in to his every feeling of vulnerability. A fighter, a warrior, a competitor, a poker player, and a lackluster lover are being developed. You have a man who feels everything, but shows little to none of it. Now his face becomes what we call "the poker face."

If I had a dollar for how many times I've heard a woman say, "I can't tell what he's thinking," I'd be set for life. Women around the world spend hours each day trying to read men. A man isn't like a book; you can't just read the words and see how the story unfolds. You have to understand a man, his history, and his biography to understand the makeup of who he is.

How many women have you seen cry in public? How many men have you seen cry in public? Other than at a funeral, I don't really see men cry in public. I went to a funeral recently, and the male family members were outside drinking alcohol and telling jokes. The father of the young lady who had died was laughing and joking with everyone. He seemed as if his child had just come into the world, not left the world. He also was drinking a few glasses of alcohol. That's how a lot of men handle their feelings. In most cases, we never let our opponent see us sweat. It's a battle tactic. If you show weakness, you've lost. That's something every man knows, and when it comes to relationships, it's a challenge. It starts out as a battle to see who will win the upper hand. Sadly, the man and the woman become opponents—not teammates. Most men enter a relationship to devour the opponent and have the woman eating out of their hands. It's not a fair game because the woman is coming to love, and the man is coming to win. We are conditioned differently.

A woman sees a relationship as an opportunity to fall in love. A man sees it as an opportunity to be sucked in and then drained of everything he's worth. Love is a beautiful thought for most women, but it's a very scary thought for most men.

In college, I was talking to one of my teammates on the football team. He told me he didn't tell his woman she was beautiful or write her poems and such because if he put her on a pedestal, she would look down on him. Is that true? Maybe so in some cases, but his goal then was to debase her and leave her wondering about his feelings. When a man does this, the mixed signals cause confusion in the woman's heart and she's constantly trying to win his love, hoping that if she does it right, he will open up and assure her that he loves her in return. The woman is now in the weaker position, working for him instead of him working for her. This tactic makes a woman feel vulnerable and inadequate. In the case of my teammate, the girlfriend didn't have a clue if he really liked her, but in fact, he loved her. He loved her, but due to being a young man and a football player, he was conditioned to not expose his emotions or feelings. He didn't want to be vulnerable to any form of attack, not even the attack of love. The fear of falling in love makes a man put up a guard and wear a poker face.

It's safe to say that I'm the complete opposite, and that's why I'm writing this book. I can actually see where my teammate is coming from because there is a certain level of complacency a human gets when he or she is praised too much. I've been in positions where I felt my love was taken for granted and expected but not fully appreciated and reciprocated. I had to walk through the very thing that so many men fear: being vulnerable. I've been there time and time again. But because I've opened up to being vulnerable, I don't know how else to be. I couldn't, at this point, hide my emotions and feelings even if I wanted to. I've trained myself to be the opposite of what most men are, and that's why most men don't understand me. But I understand them perfectly because I live in the same world and I've been under the same conditioning. I honestly feel that being vulnerable in love and relationships makes for a more real and fulfilling experience. Most men never experience real love, all because of the constant poker face.

What is the poker face? The poker face in a relationship is when a person is feeling everything possible but doesn't show any of it. A man can be deeply and madly in love to the point that he would kill for his woman but never tell the woman that's how he feels. The man can be completely wrong for everything he's said and done but will refuse to show any remorse. He can be totally at fault, but instead flips it on the woman and makes her feel crazy and guilty to the point that she apologizes for the fight *he* caused. Ladies and gentlemen, that's the poker face. I've heard one woman at my seminar call it "the Jedi mind trick." I see it all the time, and I was that man in my teenage years. Men do it because we understand the depth of a woman's emotions. We know that if we leave enough unsaid and too much tension in the air, the woman is likely to break down before us and clear the air to cut the tension. She wants peace and for things to feel as normal as possible, so she'll be the bigger person and cut to the chase to get things back to how they were. She doesn't realize that going back to how it was means the man is still playing a role of toughness, a lack of feelings and emotions; but hey, it's better than nothing.

A man will tough it out and make a woman fold the winning hand. Women fold just because men won't. The woman assumes that if he is standing his ground so strongly, he must not be in the wrong. Then the woman says to herself, *I must be crazy, insecure, emotional, and hormonal or something. What is wrong with me?* That is when the man has won the poker game. His poker face forced her to fold the winning hand. The pot goes to him because he was pot committed. He played every card he could and would have lost, but his stare down cost her the game. She breaks because she feels more deeply than he does. Sympathy, empathy, then apathy and every other -athy there is start to creep up on her, and she breaks. In a few moments, she goes through an emotional roller-coaster ride, feeling every bump, turn, dip, and swoop. Her heart is tired. Her mind is tired. She wants peace in the home, and she wants it now. He knows all of this about her because he's trained to kill. If a man has been trained to kill from the time he was a boy, how hard is it for him to manipulate a woman in a relationship? Men read faces, gestures, tones, and everything else you can imagine. Why are violent street gangs made up of men? Why are snipers on roofs around the world men? Why are the greatest fighters, warriors, and soldiers men? It's not a knock against women. It's simply that we are built differently. That has to be understood in a relationship.

What women need to understand is that men are not smarter than you. Men don't feel any less than you. Men don't think any less than you. Men are just conditioned not to show what we are thinking or feeling. I am not good at the poker face at all. My wife runs circles around me when it comes to the poker face. I understand why she's so successful at it because I'm so terrible at it. Out of the thousand poker-face contests I've had with my wife, I've won probably once. Yes, I'm terrible at it. I have to be terrible at it to be able to write this book. A winning poker-faced man wouldn't write a book like this in a million years.

Bad things happen in relationships when a woman gives up everything and folds the winning hand just because her man won't open up and communicate what he's thinking or feeling. It gets bad, and I'm always the one on the other end of the phone trying to help the woman understand what is happening during our coaching sessions.

Women are smart in ways that a man isn't and can figure things out a man can't. Use your brain instead of your heart when you're dealing with a man and getting to know him. Don't fall in love with the idea of love before you've fallen in love with the man. Don't worship a man and bend over backward for his love. Let him court you, pursue you, and love you; then you can reciprocate. Know that the poker face exists, and be aware of it. When you're right, you're right, and you know you're right. If you know you're right, why succumb to this poker face and make him right? Stand your ground and stare him down until he folds his losing hand and admits to his faults. It's the only way for a man to grow into love and become vulnerable enough for a healthy, long-lasting marriage. If he's wrong, he's wrong. Make him own up to it instead of being able to escape the consequences of being wrong. It's necessary for his growth and for the health of the relationship.

Understand this: along with the poker face comes dying on your sword. Some men are willing to die on their sword instead of surrendering to love. If that's the case, you have to let him die on his sword. I don't mean literally, of course; I mean you have to be willing to let him go if he's unwilling to grow. There is a breed of men whose egos are so big that they are trained for battle, and even against a woman in love, they won't surrender. They will fight their feelings and urges and block your attempts to pull them into love. These men will do everything in their power to avoid the feelings of love and falling for a woman. This type of man can feel love for you but refuses to fall in love with you. Why? It's because he doesn't want to be vulnerable because he equates a relationship to war.

In war, if you're vulnerable, you're open for attack. In a relationship, if you're vulnerable, you're open for love. Some men don't understand the difference because they've been raised to not trust women. A woman is an opponent coming to steal and crush his heart, not a partner coming to love and caress his heart. It depends on a man's history and biography. When you look into that, it'll help you understand why he is the way he is, and then you can move forward with him. A man who refuses to be vulnerable is looking at the relationship as a battle to win. In a relationship, that mentality is not good, but that's why you see some men keep a woman for years only to break her beyond repair. It makes no sense to a sane person that a man would drag a woman along for a decade, only to go get another woman pregnant right under the nose of his main woman. It makes no sense to a sane person that a man would allow a woman to serve him hand and foot, only to break her back as she's washing his feet with her hair. So many women have become servants to peasant-minded men posing as kings. It's weak of a man to use and abuse a woman's kindness, yet it happens every day. If a man is coming for battle, he's not coming to protect you; he's come to devour you. That is why you can't enter a relationship vulnerable and trusting. Your vulnerability and your trust must be earned. Trust is earned—not given. Everyone is a suspect, until he isn't. Humans are flawed, and that has to be understood. If you give all of yourself to someone who hasn't shown you they are worth all of you, you will be taken advantage of and used.

Understanding that most men enjoy the art of war will help women protect their hearts until a man has shown his hand. A relationship isn't a poker game. He has to show his hand. If he wants to be the head of the household and take the lead in the relationship, he has to lead with love. Leading with love means he will show his hand. He will make his intentions known, and he will show himself to be open and vulnerable to love. Vulnerability will not kill him. A man knows what he wants with and from a woman from day one. If you pay attention, those intentions will be shown soon enough. You will know what type of man you have on your hands.

Yes, some men will walk away from a good woman just because they don't want to show their hand. Those men die on their swords of ego. They are not ready for love, and therefore are unfit for love in that season—or in this lifetime. It's the nature of the world to produce some people who will not surrender to love. Be understanding of this fact, and move on with your life. You can't change anyone. You can influence a person to change, but he or she has to want to change. There are also women who channel this same poker-face energy and suffer in the same ways as a lot of men do. It's not as common, but it does exist.

If you meet someone who is not open to love, it's not worth gambling. Playing poker with your heart is a gamble that can cost you way more than you can afford. The loss will be greater than any amount of money can cover. Understand that you should never gamble with your heart beyond the point of no return. Know what you can afford to lose, and stop there. If a man wants to take you further than that point, you must stop and let the relationship go. It's not worth taking a risk that will leave you emotionally bankrupt for life. There are people who have gone beyond that point and lost it all. I've spoken to people in that position, and they tell me they will never love again or even try to love again. It's a sad thing to hear and even harder to witness, but it's a reality. A relationship can break you, and that's why it's so important to know what you're getting into before you enter. You've read the stories, you've lived some of the stories, and you've seen the others with your own eyes. It's not a game. Poker is a game you can get up and walk away from. If you go too far with a relationship, you may not be able to walk away as easily.

You can't force a person to open up and love you. If you realize that his heart is closed to love and his mind is closed to the responsibility of love, keep moving.

Sheri's Perspective

A lot of people hear my and Tony's story, and the only thing they home in on is the fact that I "changed" him from one kind of man to another. There is some truth to that, but the change came only because he desired to change and wanted to be better. I sensed that early on in our relationship, which was the only reason I even considered being in a relationship with him. People assume that any person can be changed, but it's just not the case. If someone changes because you want him to, the change will be only temporary and soon enough he will return to his old ways. The change has to be something he truly desires and wants for himself. From the very beginning, I could tell that Tony was open to love and wanted to be a husband one day and it was actually something he was pursuing, to bring stability into his life. So even though he wasn't necessarily ready to be a husband when we met, he was definitely open and looking for love.

In my opinion, during the early portion of the getting-to-know-someone phase, it's important to *really* get to know him. When you first meet someone, of course he is putting his best foot forward, and that's to be expected, but you have to dig deeper. A lot of times women are more communicative, so we spend the early portion of this phase talking about ourselves and our desires. And of course the man agrees and seems to love everything you love and it seems like a match made in Heaven. In order to get past his poker face and break down the guard he has up, you have to really get to know him. Listen more than you talk, and give him time to express himself without interruption.

The first time Tony and I really talked in person, we sat by the pool. By the pool, because I had just met him and would never allow someone into my apartment without really knowing him. We literally sat by the pool and talked for hours. I believe it was about six hours. Instead of leading every conversation, I chose to be an active listener. An active listener is definitely engaged in the conversation and does communicate an opinion about what is being talked about but chooses to listen more than talk. That did two things. One, it allowed me to really get to know Tony. When someone is allowed the opportunity to talk and express himself for that long portion of time, he begins to get past the surface topics and start talking about the things that really matter. During that time, it's important to really listen and pay attention. Pay attention to the positives and negatives, and save them in your mental notebook. They are all things that can help you decide if the relationship is right for you to pursue. I learned so much about him as a person, about his family, his dreams, his ambitions, his past, and his potential future. I listened to the way he described things and the way he spoke about his family and other important people in his life. The second thing it did (which wasn't my intention at the time) was that it made him fall in love faster than he expected. Men aren't used to being given the time to speak and express themselves. So many times, we women cut men off when they are speaking. But when they are given the time to talk and express themselves and you are actively listening and participating in the conversation, it makes them feel loved and in turn makes them fall in love with you or stay in love with you. To this day, this is a dynamic part of our relationship. As I mentioned earlier, there are many nights I stay up hours after my bedtime and actively listen to Tony and what he may be going through or any new business ideas he may have. And even though I may be tired, I know how important that is for our relationship, so I participate in the conversation and give feedback on what he is talking about.

The absolute best way to really see if a person is open to love and really ready to be an active participant in a relationship is to spend time getting to know him. Don't just get to know the good facade he presents in the initial phase, but dig deeper. Ask questions, actively listen, and make an effort. It will help you decide whether he aligns with what you are looking for. This important skill will serve you well in your possible relationship and, eventually, marriage.

KEY TAKEAWAYS

✦ Most men are conditioned to put on a "poker face" and hide their emotions.

✦ Early in the relationship, spend less time talking and more time actively listening to help open the other person up.

✦ In a relationship, trust and vulnerability are a must; if you can't have those, you have to be willing to walk away.

Chapter 6

THE 72-HOUR RULE

This rule is something my wife taught me about two months into our marriage. I've since learned that it is to be used only after a deal-breaking action takes place. You can't take a 72-hour break after every argument, but there comes a time when you may need to do so.

My wife already related her side of the story about my wanting to go back into the drug life after our marriage, but here's mine. A few weeks after I turned twenty-three, I married my wife. I come from a very regular family that was entrenched in the trappings of poverty and whose members had broken mind-sets. My friends and family members were suffering from the same things I was. We'd just had our first son, and he had been born ten weeks early. He weighed two pounds, ten ounces at birth. He was fourteen inches long. I remember it like yesterday. I was so hurt, but I didn't know how to express the pain I felt. My wife went to visit him daily, but I was working, so I could make it only at certain times. I tried to stay away, to be honest, because it hurt me too bad to see him. I wasn't open to exploring and experiencing those feelings. Being vulnerable wasn't something I wanted to be. It wasn't long before his birth that I had been running in the streets with my cousins and some new friends. Coming where I'm from as a black man, you see three options. One option is to try to become a pro athlete. The next option is to work a regular job. The third is to live the street life, selling drugs and all that comes with it. I'd tried all the options, and I was on option three. When my wife had been my girlfriend, she'd left me after a few months of dating. Then we'd bumped into each other six months later, and we'd given it another try. That time around, I'd gotten into the street life a little bit, and she told me she wasn't cool with that lifestyle. She tolerated it for a week or two and then gave me an ultimatum. I chose her. After I married her, I was still young and immature, and I thought marriage meant she was trapped. Divorced is frowned upon, so I knew I'd have to take a woman through everything imaginable before she'd leave. At least, that was what I thought.

After our son was born, I told myself I wanted to make some money. Instead of picking up a second job, I decided I'd sell a little weed. I mean, what could it hurt? It's almost legal, right? That was what I told myself. My wife found out about my decision, and she wasn't happy with it. She was bound to show me that she wasn't playing with me. We talked about it, and I had my poker face on and tried to call her bluff. I went about my business running the streets with my guys and doing what I wanted to do for a week or so. It felt like a day, but I think it was about a week. Then one night, I came home, and my wife was still out and about. She had my car that day, and I drove a Chevy Impala with twenty-two-inch rims. I was missing my baby—the car, I mean. I was livid when she got home because I felt she'd been out joyriding in my car. I was wrong. She walked in and I started an argument. I was accusing her of joyriding and cheating and everything I could think of. I was trying the Jedi mind trick because I could see she meant business when she walked in the door. I knew she meant business because she had her hair in a ponytail, she was wearing her glasses, her eyes and nose were red, and she was holding her Bible. That is the starter pack for a "we need to talk" moment. I knew what it was. She was upset that I'd decided to run the streets with the boys under the guise of making extra money for my family. She knew I missed the thrill of it and just wanted to be out there. We sat down to talk, and she reminded me that she'd told me she would not be with a man who chooses to do anything illegal. Feeling the guilt, I started yelling, and she quickly shut that down, not allowing the situation to escalate. She remained cool, calm, and collected. She told me that I would have to let the street life go or let her go. I tried to call her bluff. She got up to go into the bathroom to cry. I barged in there to finish our talk because I thought I was winning. She pushed me out of the way, and she was about to leave. Things blew up, and I was trying to hold her and stop her from leaving, but she was determined to leave. I was angry, and she was hurt. I realized quickly that she was definitely going to leave and there was nothing I could do to stop her. She told me that she had been out all day talking with her uncle and his pastor about our situation, and that enraged me because I was a grown boy, and every grown boy hates for a woman to be exposed to wise counsel. I tried to make my point and plead my case, but she told me she would rather be broke and homeless than be with a man who wants to live an illegal lifestyle. I told myself that there was no way she meant that. She showed me otherwise. I had to let her walk away. I told myself, *She'll be back.* I started calling her phone right away.

I called her nonstop, and the phone just rang and rang and rang. With each call, the rings seemed to get louder. Before I knew it, the rings sounded like fire alarms in my ear. My mind was racing, and I didn't know what was going on. I didn't know if she had run to another man or what. I tried to sit still in our empty apartment, but it felt like the walls were closing in on me. I started to feel suffocated. Then I grabbed my keys, called one of my street partners, and went to his apartment to talk. He came outside and sat in my car with me. I was sitting high on my twenty-two-inch rims, so that was one thing that consoled me. I think my wife was fed up with me about those rims, too, because they had cost me $2,200 and I had bought them right after our son was born. I'd told myself I was buying them to give my son a nice ride when he got out of the intensive care unit, as if a baby would care that his dad has rims on his car. Yes, I was ignorant. My wife let me get the rims even though we could have used the money on stuff for our son. I was still trapped in a self-destructive mind-set, and I was my own worst enemy. My wife was trying to help me, but she knew some things just weren't doable, and she had her limits. She didn't waste her time telling me how to spend my refund check from college, which was what I bought the rims with, but she sure wasn't going to let me be a petty college weed man

70

again. I didn't see anything wrong with what I was doing because everyone was smoking weed. I thought I was being a businessman and supplying the demand. I thought she'd appreciate the ingenuity, but she despised it. Sheri told me that her friend from work had just lost her child's father to prison for seven years because he had been selling drugs and that she was unwilling to support me on my path to the same fate. I knew where she was coming from, but I didn't respect it.

All of that was playing through my mind as I called her to no avail. Then finally I got an answer, and it was my wife's uncle. He talked down to me as a man would. He tried to chastise me and school me. I wasn't trying to hear the first syllable out of his mouth. There wouldn't be a man who could reach me on this issue. I needed to speak to my wife. After I shared some choice words with her uncle, he felt my drift and hung up the phone. I continued calling Sheri, but I couldn't reach her.

I looked at my clock, and it was like 2:00 a.m., and I was still calling her phone. At that point, I was obsessed with trying to reach her and couldn't quit. I'd come too far to give up. That's what I was telling myself, as if I was running a marathon or something. I looked over, and my street buddy was asleep in my car. He'd fallen asleep on me in my time of need. His woman didn't mind him selling a little weed on the side. He had a full-time job just like me, and he actually worked in the juvenile detention center. It upset me that a guy I knew had a woman who allowed him to do what he wanted to do to make money. Every guy I knew had that type of woman, so why was my woman being difficult? She's wired differently. A lot of women think they'll leave, but when faced with the task of doing so, they stay. My wife left me. She maybe had a plan all along, but I don't know. All I knew is it felt like the beginning of the end.

I woke up my buddy and told him I was going home and he could go back in the house to his wife. He gave me a few words of encouragement, and I hit the road. I went home to try to sleep. I kept calling Sheri. She wouldn't answer, and I didn't understand why. *How can you ignore your husband like that? I'm not your boyfriend; I'm your husband. I'm not only your husband; I'm the father of your only child.* I was shocked.

The sun came up not too long after I got home. The experience was so painful that I've forgotten some of the details. On day two, I had to turn to the other women in my life, my mom and sister. I called them and asked my mom if I could come over. I went to my sister's apartment and hung out with them. I took a lot of clothes because I was going to stay with them until my wife answered the phone and talked to me. I needed some comfort and sound advice. I'm not sure I received that from my mom and sister, and truthfully, I think everything I heard from anyone went in one ear and out the other. I didn't want to hear anyone's voice other than my wife's. I'm not sure I was remorseful for breaking her trust or if my ego was just hurting really badly because she'd had the audacity to leave me.

I kept calling her. I probably should have checked the record books to see how many times a man has called a woman trying to get her back. I had to be in the running. Then finally, out of nowhere, she picked up the phone and I almost fainted. It was almost like Jesus answering me on the main line. Her voice sounded like an angel in Heaven picking up the prayer line. I felt a rush of emotions that I can't even describe. I jumped right into the conversation. I don't remember what I said to her, but I remember what she said to me.

She gave me the requirements to get another chance at our marriage. She told me I would have to get anger management counseling for trying to hold her against her will when she was trying to leave. She also told me that I would have to agree to never sell anything illegal again, no matter what it was or who was doing it. In the same breath, she told me I would have to cut off my friends who were in that lifestyle, mainly my cousin who gave me the weed. Last, she told me I would have to get back in the church and start walking with God again. I agreed to everything before she got the last word out of her mouth. I was so excited to have another shot at her love. I got off the phone, jumped up, got all my clothes from my sister's place, and told them I was leaving to go see my wife that night.

I hopped on the road and drove the hour and a half to our apartment. I was back. We were giving it a second try, and I had no intention of messing up again. I had already left the street life once before, so all I had to do was not get back into it. I called my best friend and my cousin. I told them that I'd be off the grid for some time, building with my wife. I told my cousin not to call me with any more sales pitches to sell weed, and I wouldn't be back out there anymore. He was offended and upset that I'd cut him off for my woman. He was shocked because he'd never been with a woman who had any real issues with his lifestyle. I told my best friend whom I'd grown up with that I wouldn't be going to the club on the weekends anymore. He was blown away, too, but told me he understood. I distanced myself from everyone.

Deep down the Lord knew I wasn't done. There was one last thing that needed to be removed. That was my idol, my Impala on twenty-two-inch rims. While I was in the apartment with my wife, making up, someone had other plans for my car. We decided to go to Taco Bell after our long talk, and when we went outside, my car was gone. I thought I had parked it in the wrong spot, but then I looked and saw there was window glass on the ground. My car had been stolen. I was crushed. I didn't have full coverage insurance on it, so it wouldn't be replaced. My car was later found in a ditch on its belly, rims and entertainment system gone. I cried like I'd lost a family member. I was more hurt about losing my car than I was about my wife leaving me for those three days. My priorities were out of whack, and God allowed me to be touched so I'd be brought to my knees. That was the straw that broke my back. I fell to my knees in a repentant state and cried out to God. I was broken. The woman I loved had almost left me, and the thing I had worshipped was gone for good. Now I would have to find the true meaning of life and get my life in order. The next day was Sunday, and Sheri and I got up and went to church in her paid-for Honda Civic. That was a humbling ride. It felt totally different driving her Civic than it did driving the only Impala in the city with twenty-two-inch rims. At church that day, I went to the altar call, I repented my sinful life, and I vowed to live for Christ.

I call that experience "the 72-Hour Rule" because my wife was gone for three days. The power of total silence is so real because it's very hard for anyone to carry through on, especially a woman. A woman is typically so forgiving and so loyal to the man she loves that leave him hanging for three whole days isn't easy, especially, as in our case, if you've been married only three months. How many women would leave a man over his selling weed? There aren't many. I've coached women who are six-figure earners and dating street dudes. A lot of women have respectable jobs and their men are still in the streets selling drugs. It's way more common than you may realize. There are also white-collar criminals who have wives or girlfriends condoning their illegal activities. As humans, we sometimes do some stupid stuff.

The thing that happens on a 72-hour break is that the person in the wrong has time to process all that he or she has done wrong. Self-talk may be the most powerful voice we hear. In those 72 hours, I had to coach and counsel myself. I confronted myself, and I felt the sting of my actions. I evaluated my immaturity, stupidity, and ignorance. I heard every negative and positive thing I could say to myself. I felt every emotion. I was on an emotional roller-coaster ride, and those emotions taught me lessons. I had to soothe myself and calm myself down to avoid a panic attack. I was hurt. I was angry. I was bitter. I was lost. I was confused. I was doubtful. I was hopeful. I was remorseful. Every emotion out there—I felt most of them. That's the power of the 72-Hour Rule. Any contact with my wife would have ruined it. If she had texted me back, even to say, "Leave me alone," it would have ruined it. Hearing her voice mail response but not being able to speak to her really messed me up. It was like calling someone's phone after he's passed away. I didn't think about any leverage I had on her. The fact that I was the father of her only child didn't give me any comfort. Having been married only a few months and her having to divorce me so soon and be embarrassed in front of her friends and family didn't comfort me. For her to walk away at that point, for the reason she walked away, I felt she was the strongest and most determined woman in the world. I was the loser, and I'd lost the love of my life because I had been taking her for granted.

The 72-Hour Rule can't be announced. That was what made it so effective. I didn't know when it would end. It felt as if she was gone for good and the next thing I'd hear from her would be a process server bringing me the divorce papers. Had she told me she was going to leave me for three days, I would have just shut down my heart, conditioned my mind, and waited it out. I had no idea where she was or what she was doing. She didn't tell me she was taking a break. She didn't tell me where she was going. She just left, and that hit me so hard. I felt powerless. It's in a man's nature always to be in control of his environment and never to be in a vulnerable position. We hate sitting with our backs to the door, anywhere. Men hate being vulnerable and not in control of everything going on in our lives. It's a weak position to be in, but it can do so much good if it's at the right time and for the right reason.

I recommend doing this only after something major has happened and you need to send a very strong message to your partner that you're not playing games. Something this powerful can't be used all the time. It's not a mind game. It's actually a time to think whether you want to move forward with the relationship or it's time to call it quits. It's an important time for both sides to evaluate their feelings and thoughts.

If you have to do this every month, or even every year, something in your relationship is really wrong.

Those 72 hours were the beginning of change in my life. I haven't been the same man since that happened. I didn't change overnight, but it definitely started the process of real change in my life, and after about two years, I was a completely different man. I know only my side of the story. I don't know if it was hard for my wife and what she did to get through the 72 hours, so I'll find out when I read her side of the story. I've never asked her about it because it was that painful. I know it sounds drastic for the women reading this, but most men who are open and honest know exactly what I mean. We don't like to be challenged by anyone. We don't like to lose to anyone. For our power to be taken from us and then to be put into a vulnerable position—almost every man hates that space. After experiencing it, I knew that I'd never intentionally push my wife to that point again because nothing in me believed that I'd be as fortunate if she had to leave me again. I'll let my wife take it from here. I think I'm ready to read her side of the story and learn what that experience was like for her.

Sheri's Perspective

Reading Tony's side of the story, I am like, "Wow, I am a genius, lol!" but I can assure it wasn't as planned and thought out as it looked to him. I do remember that night vividly, though. Leading up to that night, I had noticed a change in Tony and his personality and behavior. I knew right away he was back in the streets. Everything about his demeanor was a dead giveaway. It made me so angry because we had talked about it when I was pregnant and I had told him that was never going to be an option for us. So when he went back, it felt like betrayal. He had started to become obsessed with his car. I had agreed to let him get the twenty-two-inch rims for his car even though we had a baby in the neonatal intensive care unit and I knew that money could be used elsewhere. Honestly, I just didn't have the energy to fight about it. That day things were brewing, he was really snappy and I was unhappy as well, so I kind of knew things were coming to a head. I had to work that day, and he insisted that I drive his car. I had a few stops to make after work and by the time I got home he was accusing me of joyriding all day, so I felt like something was going to happen. See, not only did I not want him in the street life, participating in illegal activity, but it also changed his behavior and attitude, so it was a twofold problem.

Once I got home, I prepped myself and kept reminding myself to stay calm and not let his behavior get me all worked up. He was fishing for an argument, and I immediately walked away from the yelling and went into the bathroom and locked myself in there. I gave him some time to cool down, or so I thought, but then he began banging on the door and yelling for me to come out. I realized that if I didn't leave, things were going to escalate. I came out of the bathroom, grabbed my phone charger, and proceeded to leave. He tried to hold me to prevent me from leaving, but I started fighting him and he let me go.

When I left, I didn't have a plan or know what the outcome would be. That's what anyone going through this kind of situation has to understand: you leave because you know the situation is not good for you and you deserve better, but you're not leaving with any set expectations. I didn't leave with any expectation of the relationship eventually working out; I left because I knew I needed to for me. I didn't have a set time to be away, but I knew I needed to go. I left and went to stay with family. Once I left, my phone started ringing constantly. Don't get me wrong, I loved my husband and it wasn't easy to walk away from a marriage with a baby in the NICU, but I knew we were headed down the wrong road fast. Every time he called, I felt tempted to answer the phone, but I didn't have peace about it. I put my phone under the bed, out of sight and out of mind. During my time alone, I spoke with my family, prayed, and just thought about our relationship and what it would take for us to move forward. After I hid my phone, I didn't know if he was still interested, if he was texting me saying he was done, I just knew I wasn't ready to talk to him yet and I needed to feel a peace. I also wanted to give him time to cool down and be able to have a conversation like adults, not a screaming match.

After three days, I felt a peace in my spirit. I took my phone from underneath the bed, and, as I did, he called me. I answered. I didn't yell or scream, I spoke in a calm voice and explained to him the things that would have to happen if he wanted to make our marriage work. Ultimately, it would be up to him if he felt like it was worth fighting for, but if he was, I was willing to give him a chance. I knew Tony and who he really was, and this person wasn't him. I was hoping it would be a wake-up call for him and he could be the person God called him to be. Luckily, he seemed very willing and agreed to my stipulations.

I told him we could meet later and talk in person and go from there. In our marriage, that 72 hours was life changing. It was something that needed to happen, and if it hadn't, we probably wouldn't still be married today. It is important to know your worth and be willing to stand up for it at all costs, even when you are unsure of what the outcome may be.

HOW TO IMPLEMENT THE 72-HOUR RULE

✦ Have no communication at all for 72 hours.

✦ If you aren't strong enough to see the other person's call and not answer, put your phone in a place where you won't see it.

✦ Know that the 72-Hour Rule isn't for every argument.

✦ Leave when the situation isn't healthy, not because you are trying to prove a point.

✦ Pray and ask God to give you peace for whatever the final result may be.

✦ Decide what needs to happen if the relationship is going to move forward, and after the 72 hours is up, make those things clear in a calm tone.

Chapter 7

BREAK UP TO MAKE UP

The problem with the 72-Hour Rule is that some people do it too often. It may not be 72 hours. It ends up being a whole week or more. There are people who break up for months at a time and then get back together, more than once. There are three sides to every story, as you've heard before. There's your side. There's my side. Then there's the truth. In a relationship, things can get twisted and both parties see things only from their own vantage point. There's a tug-of-war going on in the relationship, and both of you are trying to gain the best footing. If neither of you is willing to submit and be selfless, you bump heads over and over again. That is what leads to breakups. In some situations, the couple takes turns deciding who's going to leave this time. In other situations, the same person leaves every time. I'll speak to what I see most often. What I see the most in off-and-on relationships is a woman who keeps leaving a man for something he's done wrong. Sometimes this lasts for decades. I answer questions from my supporters on a daily basis, and they have always been somewhere between five and twelve years in an off-and-on *situationship*.

Here's what I see happening. In enters a grown boy who is set in his ways and wants to have his cake and eat it, too. He doesn't realize that you can't do both. If you eat the cake, it's gone. If you want to keep the cake and see it sit pretty, you can't eat it. Some men decide they want to do both, and some women let it happen. This can happen the other way around. The grown boy picks his "drug of choice" to use on the woman. It may be lying, cheating, verbal abuse, an actual drug, or something else toxic. He does it over and over, and the woman is fed up with it. He's reading her every move, and he can tell she has some weaknesses in her defense. He exploits them. If there is insecurity in her, he senses it. There may be some desperation in her, and he notices it. She may be addicted to the idea of love and willing to do anything for it, and he can tell. There are all types of things going on in the mind of a woman, and if any of them is a weakness, a grown boy can sniff it out like a Thanksgiving dinner, and he's ready to feast on her insecurities to feed his own. Most of the time, women don't realize what a man can see in them. We are all glass windows, and if anyone is actually looking, it's easy to see right through us.

A woman may put up with acts of immaturity for quite some time before standing up for herself and deciding to leave. My wife told me she watched her mother walk away from a relationship, and that's what taught her it's best to walk away if you're not being treated the way you deserve to be. That's why my wife found the strength to walk away from me when she did. Nearly every relationship will go through some type of breakup at some point because it's in a man's nature to get everything he can out of a woman. It might not be a physical breakup but a season of distance or reevaluation.

When the woman finally gets fed up and decides to walk away, the man starts begging and pleading for another chance. He does and says everything perfectly. Finally she gives in and takes him back. He's an angel for a few months, typically, and then he's back to the same games. The problem is that now the soul tie is stronger and the woman is in deeper. In this get-back session, the man may do something to strengthen the tie, like move in together, get a lease in both their names, or get her pregnant, and now she feels even more trapped. Maybe they bought a house together or both of them put their names on the papers at a rental spot. The man will usually do something that he's allowed to do by the woman to tie the knot a little tighter. There's so much at stake and a lot to lose. The man gets back to his games, figuring his woman is in too deep. If she doesn't know how to swim, she will have to stay with him, and that's what happens in a lot of cases.

She reads a book like this, gets pumped up, and leaves him again. Because she's left before, he knows what it will take to get her back. He does all of that and a little more, but not too much. He doesn't want to set the bar too high because he has every intention of failing again. It's a game now. It's about ego and competition at this point—not about love and concern. No man wants to be alone, but no man wants to be the perfect man, either. In this type of *situationship*, whatever the man can get away with, he will. It's no different from a child, a dog, or any other breathing being. As a living being with a brain, if a person can get away with something, he or she will take every inch of grace given to him or her. We do it to God. We do it to our bosses at work. We do it to our spouses. Whatever is accepted, that's what is given. It's human nature in most cases. I wish the exceptions to the rule were greater in number, but that's not the case.

The man comes back a second time, and this time, he may be perfect for a year. He needs to build up some more vacation time before asking to take off again. He does everything right and even puts in the extra hours. Just when the woman is falling back in love and thinks he's a changed man for good, boom! He hits her yet again with another surprise. It's too much. It's too deep now. The relationship has been going on four to five years at this point, and it's too far down the road to turn back. The woman is exhausted, but she feels stuck. She's gotten to know the man so much, given everything of herself, and thinks she doesn't have any other options. He has her right where he wants her, down and out, feeling destitute and without an escape. Of course, it's not the true reality of the situation in most cases, but that's what she's telling herself and that's what he wants her to think. If a man can get you to the point where you feel out of options and he's your only option, you have to accept what he's willing to give you. Millions of couples are in this very situation today and calling it "normal." That's not love. I know this for a fact more than anyone else because I'm deep in the trenches every day. That's why I'm doing this work, because I see the reality of what we call love today. There's always a light at the end of the tunnel, but most people in a toxic situation feel trapped.

It's draining to think about starting over from scratch, getting to know someone else, and building trust. It's a scary thought. That's what keeps most people in toxic *situationships*. It's always easier said than done, and that's what people tell themselves to keep them in it. The men or women who are doing the damage in the relationship will read this and try to rip the book in half. All of a sudden, this is the worst book ever written and I ought to be stoned alive for writing such garbage. That's the defense men take against me online. Those are some of the words I read from men who aren't ready to grow and change for the better. I know I don't tell any lies about this stuff, but I'm still called every name in the book. I let it roll off of me because I know what it's like when you have a sword of truth and you're in spiritual warfare. The spirits we wrestle with are not flesh and blood. It's so real and the truth is so deep that it's hard to hear. To think someone is going through this type of drama is hard to accept. It's even harder when it's your own situation.

After the third time a woman takes a man back, or vice versa, it's pretty much a wrap for a shot at a healthy relationship. It becomes like the boy who cried wolf. The offender no longer believes the victim is serious about standing up for himself or herself. It's an all-out attack at that point. Something drastic has to happen to the person in the wrong for him or her to come to the realization about how damaging his or her actions are. You've seen in the movies where a man takes a woman for granted for a decade. Then he gets into an accident that leaves him crippled, and now, all of a sudden, he realizes she's the greatest thing that has ever happened to him, or he loses it all financially, and she's still by his side. Art imitates real life. Those stories are written from the lives I'm coaching every day. I kid you not, sometimes I feel like throwing up from some of the stories I hear. I was toxic as a young man, and I'm still left speechless by some of the things I hear. If your mind can imagine it, I've heard it. Listen to what I just said: if your mind can imagine it, I've heard it.

This emotional roller-coaster ride makes you lose all your food. Everything you stood for is out the window when you are in a "break up to make up" relationship. It's no longer a relationship; it's a *situationship*. You're being used and abused at every turn. I believe most offenses in love are forgivable. No one is perfect, and at some point, we all need a second chance. A second chance is almost a given in every relationship. It's the third, fourth, and fifth chances where you start to lose all self-respect and dignity. The person who is coming into and going out of your life loses all respect for you. You keep saying there's a wolf about to eat the other person alive, and every time he or she looks up, it's a sheep coming to cuddle. That leads you up to the time you actually have to be the big bad wolf and say enough is enough. The other person doesn't know how to take it because you've said you were done so many times. At some point, you don't even believe yourself anymore. You leave, knowing that as soon as you walk away, you'll be back. I coach so many people who have left a relationship and are sitting still waiting for the person who dogged them out to come back. It confuses me, but I try to understand it. Women write me daily and tell me they left their man and they're wondering when he will come back and beg for forgiveness. It's almost like no one leaves to leave. People leave to be chased, and that's the problem.

In a relationship, there are no breaks. When I say "breaks," I mean breakups. You have to decide if you're going to *work through it to-*

gether or you're going to *let it go*. If you keep breaking up and calling it a "break," your relationship loses all momentum and you have to keep starting over every time you get back together. You start over and build right back up to the same point of breaking up again. So many couples I've coached have been off and on for fifteen years. I don't know what it is about year fifteen that makes people really start to sit and think about how much of their life has been wasted on this roller coaster with someone who has no intention of changing. At that point, the offender is complacent. You've taught him or her how to speak a relationship language with you, and it's being spoken so fluently that anytime things get intense, it comes out again. If it's lies, abuse, cheating, whatever it is, it keeps coming up.

My wife gave me a second chance in dating and a second chance in marriage. I don't count them as the same thing because they came in two different seasons of our lives. Different circumstances and situations dictate different responses. During the dating phase, she broke up with me after a few months. It felt like two months to me, but it could have been three or four months. I'll tell you what I think, but she may say otherwise. I think it's because her ex was begging her for another chance and she'd been with him for a year, so it was tough to just throw away that history. On top of that, I wasn't treating her right. I was being controlling, jealous, and insecure, and she was like "We need to take a break." She didn't break up with me directly, but she said we need to take a break. I was so arrogant and stuck in my ways that I said, "Forget you," and I moved on with my life and didn't contact her once for six months.

Eventually, I contacted her because one of my friends wanted to be connected with her roommate. I reached out to her on instant messenger and asked her if she could set it up. She said she would. On the day my friend was supposed to come, he didn't show up. I reached out to her and told her that he hadn't shown up, so could I still come visit with her anyway. She said yes. As we were standing outside her apartment talking, I realized that she'd given her ex a second chance but it had lasted only about two months of the six that we had been apart. He hadn't actually changed, so she had kicked him to the curb and was single again. For myself, my ex had taken me back, and I hadn't changed for her, either. I was still toxic. But when I found out my Sheri would give me another shot because she had cut me out of her life so quick the first time, I wanted to get it right. I avoided all the things that had gotten me the ax the first time around and was looking for new things to get away with. She found the new things I was into and shut them down, too. Because I knew she was going to be my wife the first time we dated, I wasn't going to let her get away this time. I was taking it all the way to marriage this time. We were married ten months later. I told you about the second chance she gave me in marriage, and that time, it was because we'd had a child, we'd just gotten married, and my offense wasn't against her but against my purpose and destiny. She forgave me for hurting myself and God, and she gave me one more chance. I was smart enough to know that if a woman would leave me because of those two things, if I did something serious like cheat on her or become abusive, she'd leave me for good, without question.

You teach people how to treat you by what you allow, what you stop, and what you reinforce. If you keep walking away from a relationship but you stand still and letting the other person come into and go out of your life, you're losing yourself. Your partner doesn't respect you, and you're hurting yourself more than helping yourself. There's a fine line between loyalty and stupidity. You have to know what side you're walking on. In baseball, it's three strikes and you're out. Then it's three outs and your whole team is out. Why do you give so many strikes and outs in real life? This isn't a game. Your heart is on the line, and a heart isn't to be played with. If you're going to fight for the relationship, agree to fight for it together. But to keep breaking up only to make up again and again, you're wasting your life away and that time won't be given back.

Some people pride themselves on having a relationship that has endured countless breakups. That's not a reason to be proud. That's something to be ashamed about, but ashamed to the point of change. There's nothing cool about being used and abused several times by the same person. Yes, you've gone through a lot and you deserve a lot better, but don't settle. Make up your mind. If a person keeps pushing you away, that means he or she doesn't value your heart or your time. Understand that, and stop trying to stretch a season into a lifetime. By stretching that season, you'll end up in the winter with your summer clothes on, about to freeze to death. You have to open your eyes and recognize when a relationship has run its course. It's called dating for a reason. You're supposed to try it out and be okay with walking away if it doesn't work. It's marriage that you're supposed to fight for, and at that point, you should know who you have. But even in marriage, it's not smart to put yourself into an unsafe situation multiple times.

Pay attention to the signs, and be honest with what the other person is telling you. If it's time to throw in the towel, save your sanity and do so. There is love on the other side of that relationship. It's never too late to start over fresh, heal, and attract real love from someone who deserves you. It doesn't matter how many kids, how many years, and how many memories you have together. Just because you have a history with someone doesn't mean you have a future with him or her. If the person is meant to be in your life and stand the test of time, it will be evident. Your circumstances and situation will line up perfectly, and it'll make sense to give it another go. If that's not the case, accept it and move on. Breaking up and making up countless times is never the route to go.

Sheri's Perspective

During that 72 hours away from Tony, I spent most of the time alone. I didn't really want to hear anyone's opinion during that time. I prayed, cried, and did a lot of thinking. I knew I needed to hear God, and I prayed for peace and understanding. I didn't realize it at the time, but I was creating a set of rules for something that could change the face of relationships.

Here are the rules I created.

THE RULES

Know Your Worth

Before you enter into a relationship, determine what your standards are and love yourself enough to stick to them.

Don't Leave Just to Leave

The 72-Hour Rule isn't something you should implement during every argument or disagreement. When you decide to leave, it could very well be forever, so leave with that in mind.

Take Time to Think

Use your time away in a healthy way. If you leave and run to your friends to gossip, not only are you going to get bad advice, you are going to cloud your judgment. Use your time away to pray and to spend time with your own thoughts and feelings. During that time, you can evaluate your relationship and make sure that there is more good than bad in it and it's worth fighting for.

Know That It's Called a "Second Chance" for a Reason

So many people leave their relationships only to go back over and over again. If offenses are occurring over and over again that warrant your leaving, you need to reconsider the viability of your relationship. If a person hasn't made the necessary changes after you gave him or her another opportunity, he or she may not be the person for you.

Stay Calm, Cool, and Collected

Nothing is accomplished by screaming. Be able to vocalize your desires and expectations in a tone that allows your significant other to listen to and process what you're saying. If you are screaming, it causes him or her to shut down and not really take in what you are asking of him or her.

Understand That a Happy Ending Isn't Guaranteed

When you decide to leave, the other person may not want to fight for the relationship or for you, and you have to be okay with that. Leave because you know you deserve better and you love yourself enough to recognize that. You aren't leaving to prove a point or to get the upper hand. As they say, if you play with fire you will get burned; that applies here as well. If you leave for the wrong reasons and motives, nine times out of ten, things won't work out forever.

Chapter 8

SHOW, DON'T TELL

One of the most powerful things my wife has done is show me what she means instead of telling me what she means. She lives by example, and that has taught me how she wants to be treated. Recently, we were in a mall at the food court and my wife was standing in line to get food while I went to the restroom. When I came back, she told me about this lady who was talking very disrespectfully to her husband. She said the husband had been coughing from an apparent sickness and the wife had started cursing at him. The wife had been calling him dirty names and told him to get up and get away from her because she didn't want to be around his disgusting self. Then my wife said, "I don't understand how a woman could talk to her man like that and then be confused when he cheats on her and leaves her." My wife has never once yelled or cursed at me—never. It's the most powerful thing ever. You've heard the saying "The loudest in the room is the weakest in the room." Men really believe that. It's also been said, "You have to watch out for the quiet ones because they are crazy."

On the one hand, it's respected how my wife deals with me. On the other hand, it's kind of scary, to be honest. Because she doesn't yell, curse, posture, and act tough, it leads me to believe that she's really not about the games. She's all business when things get serious, and there's no tough talk.

By her not yelling and cursing at me, it's kept my respect for her intact. There is one thing a man needs more than anything else, and that's respect. If you disrespect a man, it's over for you. God forgives; men rarely do. I tell women all the time that if you're cursing your man out, he might go cheat on you for silent revenge. A man will sleep with another woman and never tell you for his own satisfaction and revenge. It happens every day. Women think they are winning the battle by outtalking a man and being a wordsmith. No; he's letting you talk tough, and then he's doing you dirty. Men don't let anything slide. Either you pay now, or you pay later. Different men get revenge in different ways, and most of the revenge, we take to the grave. I don't think women know that, or else there would be a lot more showing instead of telling and yelling.

One thing about all men is for sure: we respect action. Although it hurts, we'd rather a woman walk out of our lives to make her point than yell at us and curse us out. Yelling and cursing don't hurt a man. They're disrespectful, but they don't hurt him; they anger him. A lot of women throw low blows with words, hoping the man will feel the same pain that she felt when he cheated on her. That's not the case. A man may laugh in a woman's face when she's yelling and cursing. To most men, it's like a little puppy barking at a big rottweiler. Unless a woman's craziness is certifiable on paper, a man doesn't fear her. It's just not in a man's nature to fear a woman because of how God created us. I mean no disrespect, but it's just not common.

Women ask me all the time why successful and strong women intimidate men. I tell them that no man is intimidated by a woman; he just doesn't want to be with her. A homeless man will shoot his shot at Beyoncé if she walks past him, and if she will give him a chance, he will take her up on it and love her as if he was a millionaire himself. He's not going to pass up the opportunity because of her money and success. I say that to say, when you're yelling and cursing at your man, you're wasting your breath and running up your blood pressure for no good reason. It doesn't scare him, it doesn't get your point across, it doesn't hurt him, and it doesn't help the situation. All it does it anger him and makes him want revenge for feeling disrespected. There is power in a calm answer. To be slow to anger is to be emotionally intelligent, and that is respected.

I can't disrespect my wife at this stage in my life because she's never disrespected me. I know she doesn't fear me at all. I'm only a couple inches taller than she is, and she's just about as strong as me. I strike no fear into her at all. She doesn't yell because she doesn't want to be yelled at, and she knows it's a waste of her energy. She possesses class and dignity, and to get out of character and yell and curse would be beneath her. When you know who you are, you don't stoop to the immature level of others. Instead, you elevate them to yours.

I've fallen deeper in love with my wife over the years, and when I look back and remind myself that she's never slapped me in the face, called me something other than my name or "babe," or yelled at me, it melts my heart. It makes me feel loved and respected. It also makes me hold my wife in high regard because I realize that her queenlike behavior lets me know I chose the right woman.

There's a communication difference between men and women. Women are more articulate and expressive in most cases. Listen to a four-year-old girl talk, and listen to a four-year-old boy talk. There's a drastic difference in most instances. The female brain develops faster and better in that area. That's why some men say you'll never beat a woman in an argument. It's scientific. It takes a special man to beat a woman in a verbal argument. What happens when men get into verbal altercations? They get abusive. They turn into verbal abuse or physical abuse. If you back the wrong man into a corner with your words, he's going to attack you. Some of you know how it goes when men feel attacked. It's not pretty, and the things that are said or done can't ever be unsaid or undone. The beauty of not attacking with words is that you give yourself a chance to de-escalate the situation. Think back to middle school, when arguments would break out between two boys or between two girls. The two girls could argue for five minutes, and it just might go to blows. With the boys, two words might be said and fists would be flying. We are wired differently. A man respects actions—not words. I'm a life coach for pro athletes. They tell me often, in so many words, that the only thing they will respect from me is what they've seen me do. They see me love my wife and how I treat her, and that's why they want relationship advice from me. They do not want a single syllable of advice from me about their sport because I've never played their sport as a pro. Men respect action. If you're talking and yelling, there's no respect there.

The very first time I tried to yell at my wife, she put her hand up and told me not to talk to her like that. It was like she was calming a storm at sea with the raising of her hand. I was shocked because a woman has never calmed me in that way. She didn't shrink like most women do when a man is yelling at them. She didn't yell back like some other women do. She remained calm and raised her finger up to my eye level, and she sternly said, "Don't talk to me like that." She was like Cesar Millan training a dog. She got me right there, and I've never yelled at her since that day. Why? Because I respected her approach and it made me respect her as a person. She showed me by example how to have an adult conversation without yelling and acting like a fool. A man will act up or act out if you do too much talking. Acting up means he's going to match or top your energy. Acting out means he's going to take it out on you some other way.

Have you seen the movie *Tag*? It's about adult men who've been playing a game of tag for something like thirty years. That movie is a loose depiction of how men really are. We have to get the last lick or the last word in. The last blow has to belong to the man, and it's extremely hard for most men to be the bigger person and not do something to get revenge. He may be absolutely quiet and not yell or curse back at you, but he's going to do something to get even. I'm speaking of the majority; of course, I know there are emotionally intelligent men who don't have to act up or act out. How many do you know personally? How many have you dated? Are you with one now? It's not as common as we need it to be, but I believe we will get there.

I've watched these relationship dynamics play out for over a decade now. I see a lot of hurting women masking their anger with violence. It may be verbal violence, and sometimes it's physical violence. There are women who will try to fight their man in a physical fight or dare him to hit her just to prove a point. That attention-seeking behavior is dangerous, and it doesn't end well. My wife has never once tried to fight me physically, no matter how mad I may have made her.

I have coaching calls with couples, and the man tells me the stuff the woman has said to him. Then the woman tells me stuff she's said to the man. Sometimes I almost drop the phone. I know right then that the man is sleeping with every woman who will have him, but I can't say that on the phone and start a fight during the coaching session. I let it play out, and then the guy ends up attributing his actions outside the relationship to the way his woman disrespects him with her words. The woman then says, "Yeah, I know I have a foul mouth." Some women know it and take pride in it because they think they are getting even with a man or bringing him to his knees. Little does a woman like that know that she's creating her worst enemy, and then, from that day forward, she'll be sleeping with the enemy. I listen to them and watch to see how things play out.

I've always heard people say, "Respect is due a dog." It's slang for "Even a dog deserves respect." What it means is that if you respect a dog, you should definitely respect a human being. As you think about it, most of us talk nicer to dogs than we talk to some people. How do you talk to your dog when you're mad at the dog? It's probably still nicer than how you speak to your partner when you're mad at him or her.

My wife doesn't entertain arguments. She doesn't entertain my mood swings. She sidesteps power struggles, and I'll see her back, walking away, before I hear her mouth arguing. If I'm in a bad mood because I woke up too early, she doesn't stoop to my level and check me about my attitude. She sidesteps it and goes on as if she didn't even notice. That gets me out of my mood real quick.

Another thing I see her do is get over stuff very quickly. I've done some stupid things over the years, and because she decided to forgive and forget, she did just that, and I never heard about it again. She made a grown-woman decision to forgive me for whatever stupid thing I said or did, and she doesn't bring it up again. She moves on and never mentions it during our next disagreement. That's her showing me what forgiveness looks like, not telling me what she forgave me for doing. If you keep telling your partner what you've had to forgive him for, you haven't actually forgiven him. You're holding on to a grudge, and your relationship is going to be stagnant because of it. There are many men who do this as well. It can go either way. I've been guilty of it, too.

A long time ago, we decided not to argue but instead to discuss. If it's not worth breaking up over, it's not worth arguing over. That's our slogan when it comes to arguments. We have disagreements and we have discussions, but not arguments with yelling, name-calling, and storming off. Discussions can be firm, stern, and serious without being disrespectful. My dignity and self-respect have remained intact through my relationship, and I'm grateful for that. When hearing some of the things men and women have told me their partners have said to them, I've been blown away several times. I'd rather see my wife walk away from me than hear her try to rip me to shreds with her words. I can respect her walking away, but I can't respect a verbal attack.

This applies to more than just verbal communication. You also have to show how you want to be loved. I love physical touch. When my wife rubs my back, head, neck, or anything else, it gives me the chills. She's not very touchy. She loves to hold hands and things like that, but she's not an overly touchy type of person. Me, on the other hand, if she's in arm's reach, I'm rubbing, massaging, or squeezing whatever I can get my hands on. In the store, I walk behind her and massage her shoulders. While I'm driving, I reach over and massage her neck and shoulders with one hand. If we're sitting on the couch, I'm playing in her hair and massaging her head. My showing her how I like to love makes her do the same for me. I've noticed her going out of her way to massage my neck or play in my beard and massage my face. It's not her personality, but by me showing her how good it feels, she wants to return the feeling. I could sit and complain about what she's not doing for me all day, or I can lead by example. She loves to hug. She would stop in front of me and say, "Hug me." It would annoy me so bad because she would say it in a tone that said, "You never hug me." I started telling her, "If you want a hug, then hug me and I'll hug you back, but I don't need hugs, so I don't think to hug you." So now, instead of complaining about my lack of hugs when I'm passing by her in the house, she just steps in front of me and hugs me. She will literally stand there and hug me for five minutes if I let her. I'm claustrophobic, so I try to wiggle out after about one or two minutes. I still appreciate the doing instead of the telling, though. Men respect doing, and I believe women do, too. Of course, some things have to be said and talked about, but after that, it's about action.

If you get too caught up in nagging, complaining, fussing, fighting, and arguing, you will lose your relationship. It's been said more than once that a surefire way to lose a man is to nag at him all the time. Men may be immature at times, but we are very smart. You actually don't have to tell us something more than once if we love and respect you. Once you've shown us and stated what you need and expect, we can do it. If a man doesn't reciprocate the love you give him or doesn't give you the type of love and respect you ask for, there is a major problem with the relationship. Don't overlook the fact that your man isn't giving you what you need even after you give him the love he needs. I believe men should lead in love, but sometimes a woman has to lead in specific areas. There are certain parts of relationships, like quality time, affection, and communication, that may not come as easily to some men. It's okay for a woman to lead by example and show what they mean.

I've learned more about my wife's idea of communication over the years. She could bark at me and complain that I don't talk to her, but instead, she just starts talking to me. If we take turns talking, I'll mention business and she will mention something that's interesting to her. Our conversation will be a business topic from me, then a YouTube vlogger topic from her. She will talk with me about anything business I want to talk about and as long as I want to talk about it. Then, when it's her turn to talk, she will bring up something related to our sons or something she saw online. I may not really respond to it and may take the conversation back to business. She could shut down and flip out, but she goes right back to her YouTube or Instagram topic. She's had to tell me a time or two about this, but in a cool and calm way. She may say a sentence about it, and then she keeps it moving. I learn from her example, and it has taught me that not every conversation has to be about a kingdom issue. It's okay to relax and just shoot the breeze about some meaningless stuff in life. I realize our interests are different, our responsibilities are different, and our lives are different. I want to talk about mine, and she talks with me about it. She wants to talk to me about hers, and I have to respect that and talk to her about hers. When I've made an effort to be very interested about the blogger she's telling me about, she lights up like a Christmas tree. It's the cutest thing. I don't understand it all, but because I love her, I try to get into it. It's amazing how she can be genuinely interested in what I have to talk about, though. I learn from the communication skills that she exhibits, when instead, she could be using her skills to put me down and make me feel bad for not being able to converse on her level. She's *showing* instead of *telling*, and that has made all the difference in her influence in my life.

Sheri's Perspective

I am very much a believer in the "Treat others like you want to be treated" mantra. It's a cliché, I know, but it's definitely part of my core belief system. I believe it also applies in a relationship, of course in big things like cheating but also in small things like the way you speak to each other. From the very start of our relationship, I made sure that I showed Tony as much respect as possible because those are the same standards of respect that I expect from him.

I hear a lot of women speaking to their husbands, and I am literally flabbergasted. I can't believe they speak in the tone they do or even with the words coming out of their mouth. I don't think in the course of our dating season and our marriage, I have ever yelled or screamed at Tony, and I definitely have never called him any derogatory names in any form. It's not because I am intimated by him or fearful of him in any way, it just comes down to respect. In the very beginning of our relationship we were having a discussion and he began to raise his voice and I immediately told him not to raise his voice at me. I wanted to show him what I expected from him in our relationship right away. You can't expect one thing and then treat someone the opposite of that; it's a two-way street.

Having mutual respect for each other really helps our relationship flourish in many ways. Imagine having an argument where neither party is yelling or cutting the other off. Both are actively listening and speaking in calm tones. Guess what? You are not arguing, you are having a discussion. It's so much easier to process what someone is saying when you are speaking kindly and in love. When people ask us about our arguments and we tell them we don't argue, it's because we actually don't. We have discussions, but we never argue. When we speak like this, we are both able to see where the other person is coming from, and we figure out a way to meet in the middle.

Our society is used to watching drama and reality television, so some people assume that if you are not fussing or cussing, you're not in a relationship. I promise you, that's not the case. It's not normal to be arguing every day. It's not normal to be screaming and yelling. It's not normal to call each other names. It's not normal to slam doors in each other's faces. When you learn to live in a way in which both people show and receive respect, you realize a new normal and it's a beautiful thing.

KEY TAKEAWAYS

+ Lead by example, show respect, and don't settle for being treated with disrespect.

+ Don't yell, scream, and nag; have conversations, not arguments.

+ Show how you want to be loved, and your partner will reciprocate.

Chapter 9

THE RULES OF ENGAGEMENT

I'm often asked how to date in today's society. One thing is for sure, and that is the fact that principles don't change. Class is class. Respect is respect. Dignity is dignity. It doesn't matter if it's 1440 or 2040; principles don't change. Yes, our values change in society. Our morals change in society. But some things will always be the same. If you ask a grown man and a grown boy the same question, you'll get two different answers. If you ask a man who wants to sleep with you and a man who doesn't want to sleep with you the same question, you'll get two different answers. There are men who are influencers who will lie to women about how men think because they are still playing the game. If a man is still sleeping with multiple women, you can't take his advice on relationships. He won't tell you the entire truth because then you'll see his games from a mile away. He shoots himself in the foot by telling the whole truth. I'm 100 percent faithful to my wife, so I don't have to hide any truth. I'll tell the truth even if it hurts you. My truth isn't just my truth. My truth comes from seeing thousands of case studies and also having firsthand experience. Sometimes people want to argue with me because they've seen three exceptions to the rule. Congratulations. There are at least three people who have hit a tree at ninety miles per hour and lived. Are you going to try it, too? No. We don't base life on exceptions to the rules. We live by the rules. That being said, I'm going to share with you the rules of engagement, as I believe they should be. Take these rules and put them up against your own experience and a few of your friends'. See if you made any of these mistakes and how they turned out for you. Then ask yourself if you've ever done it like I'm about to tell you.

I'll start by saying that I myself am an exception to the rule. I'm honest with myself, and I know that things rarely work out the way they worked out for me. But I believe I was graced because God has a calling on my life. He has allowed me to get to this point in my life to write this very book, and hopefully, He will allow me to write the thirty or forty others I have in mind for you. By the time He calls me home, I hope to have written the largest collection of love and relationship books known to man. Being an exception to the rule, you'd think I would teach the exceptions, but no, I teach the rules. I had to make every mistake and do it all wrong so I'd know what I'm talking about when I talk about the rules. The best teacher is experience.

DATING

Dating today is a mess. A lot of women tell me they hate dating. Men love it. A woman's frustration and/or desperation sometimes causes her to jump into bed with a man, trying to hurry and get to the point of the relationship for him, so he will make it exclusive and give her something real. That desperation is a killer. The woman gets used and played like a deck of cards, and the man is off to the next woman. Now the woman is even more angry and frustrated because once again, she's slept with a man and it went nowhere. I've noticed that the older a woman gets, the quicker she is to hop into bed with a man. It's actually harder for a man to sleep with a woman in her early twenties than it is for him to sleep with a woman in her thirties or forties. A woman who has lived that life will have to tell you why; I'm just reporting from the male experience.

Sex happens way too soon in dating today. Imagine being in a track meet, and you're about to race. You walk up to the starting line, and you're going through your routine. You crouch to get into your stance for the start of the race. As you begin to lift your head up to look ahead, the referee walks up to you. He stretches his arms toward you, holding out a shiny gold medal. You look at him with a very confused face, and you reach out slowly to grab the medal. He then places a ribbon around your neck with the gold medal on it. You're totally confused at this point, but then he tells you "Congratulations" because you've won the race. Yes, you won the race, and it hasn't even started. Are you still going to run? No. It makes no sense to exert energy to do so because you're already the winner. All of your training is a waste at this point. You go to five more races, and the same thing happens. This is getting ridiculous. You're training for a race—a marathon— but you're awarded the gold medal before you even get started.

Ladies, that's what it's like to be a man dating today. It's so easy. Men are prepared for a marathon, but the sex happens so soon and so easy that the race is won before it's started. I know a lot of women say it's the man's fault and he shouldn't have asked if that wasn't what he wanted. I wish it were that way, too, but it's not, so you have to adapt. As a woman you have to realize that you have the final say. The "yes" belongs to you. It's yours to give. The "no" also belongs to you. It's yours to give. The man is entering your life to run a marathon of love. If you bow out and give him the prize before he's started the race, you lose. He wants to run the race. The man is coming for challenge. He's looking for love, and he expects to have to work for it. In most cases, he's asking you for the prize before the race to determine if the race is worth running. If you're one of the women who gives the prize before the race even begins, he will take it, but he won't respect you. He will move on, and he will be looking for a woman who is going to make him run the marathon and work for her love. Every man knows that to capture a woman's heart, it's of the essence that he works. He is conditioned to work, and he's ready to work. Just because he asks doesn't mean he wants what you're about to give him. He's just checking to see if you know your value.

Have you ever found a steal at a pawnshop or vintage store? You may pick something up, and you immediately know the value because you've studied the brand or company that makes it. Your eyes light up, and you're so excited. You take the item up to the counter and ask the clerk how much it costs. She scans the tag, and it's 90 percent cheaper than what you were expecting. You try to keep cool and pretend you're thinking about it. All the while, you're about to explode on the inside. You know the worth of the item, but the pawnshop doesn't, so it gives it away for cheap. The same thing is happening in our dating world today. Women don't realize their value, and men take advantage of that. If you know your value, a man will give you what you're worth. If you don't know your value, he will give you what you'll accept. A man won't give you more than you think you're worth, because then he'd feel like he's playing himself. On the other hand, he will give you all that you feel you're worth because you determine your value—not him. If he wants to be with you, he will do what it takes to have you.

Dating should look like this: The man should initiate contact every day. If a guy is interested in a woman, he will not let a day pass without contacting her. He will contact her throughout the day by text, but he will also ask for a time they can speak on the phone. His goal is to be on her mind all day long. He texts when she's not available to talk, and then he finds the time to talk in person when she can. He won't let a day pass unless he literally is undersea or out in space and can't reach her. That is what an interested grown man will do. Anything other than that diminishes his commitment as a man, and it's a sign that there are other distractions. Those distractions could be anything.

If you live close to each other and work normal jobs, he will make sure he takes you on a date at least once a week. By close, I mean within an hour apart. A man who really likes you will drive up to four hours one way to see you. Yes, that's an eight-hour trip. Oh, yeah! I'm serious. This is the level of work a man will put in when he's serious. We work for what we want. Women think it's crazy and don't know what to expect because they get so accustomed to dating men who don't really like them. A man who really likes a woman will go above and beyond.

If a man is truly interested in a woman, he will avoid sexual discussions. He will get to know you first, and then he will ease his way into the other stuff. If he receives any pushback, he will shut it down and go back to the pure and clean talk. He's going to test the waters, though, just to see how much value the woman has put on her body and her mind. He's ready and willing to work. He just wants to know that she knows her own value.

For the woman in the equation, things are little different. She is the decider. It's up to her to confirm or deny the man's interest. If she's not interested in the man, she needs to make that clear up front so he can move on with his life. He's a grown man; he's heard worse. He can handle it. If the woman is interested, she needs to subtly make it known through reciprocation. That means if he's initiated contact three days in a row, the next day, the woman should initiate contact. Then she should allow the man to initiate the next three days and alternate with an approximately three-to-one ratio. It doesn't have to be exact but as close as possible. The three-to-one ratio is like the mile markers and the water stations in a marathon. It allows the man to work for the woman, but it also assures him that the work is not in vain.

When it comes to the actual dates, the woman shouldn't assume anything. She should offer to pay her half of the bill. If he declines her offer, she should accept graciously. For a woman not to offer to pay her half tells the man that she's a taker and may be with him only for free food. If she offers to pay the entire bill, that tells the man that she's insecure and/or desperate and trying to prove a point. Offering to pay her half tells the man that she's not a taker and she brings something to the table. Then, by allowing him to decline her offer, it tells the man that although she's independent, she's mature and ready to become interdependent. To be interdependent is to be ready for marriage. A man reads into all of this, even if he can't articulate what he's processing.

Some men may allow the woman to pay the entire bill, which is a red flag. It says that he's a taker and will use the woman. Other men will decline the woman's offer and pay the entire bill. That doesn't mean much because it's technically what he's supposed to do. It could mean he's a real man—or a real player. The woman will have to keep her eyes on him. Some men may allow the woman to pay her half. That is also a mixed message because it means either that his funds are tight or that he respects her independence and doesn't want to step on her toes. Last, it could mean he's dating around and wants to keep his expenses to a minimum because she's not the only woman he's taking on dates. He will respect her for offering to pay her half nonetheless.

As you can see, nothing is clear cut. You have to keep your eyes open and pay attention to the signs. Dating should be daily conversations that last up to an hour on the phone and then at least one physical date each week. If the relationship is long distance, the date should be a FaceTime or Skype date every week. You'll have to be creative, like being on the phone and watching a Netflix movie together.

Dating should not involve sex, although so many people I coach don't heed that advice. Sex is too risky today. You're adding to your soul ties, increasing your body count, and decreasing your chances of marriage. It's not wise to have sex before marriage. Also, if you're a Christian, you know it's also a sin against both God and your body. If God values your body in that way, you should, too. Most of us make bad choices. I made the bad choice to have sex before marriage over and over again. I thank God I made it here to tell about it. Today I'm coaching a lot of people with sexually transmitted diseases and children out of wedlock, and these are some tough situations. It's all because of premarital sex. Premarital sex isn't even that good, and it doesn't really do anything for you. It's a soul tie for no reason, really. It makes sense only when you're in love with the person and you've made a commitment until death does you part. It's a hard road, but I have to recommend it because it's your safest and smartest bet in the world today.

A lot of people move in together. It's a mistake. The goal should be to fall in love—not to live together. If you fall in love with and marry each other, moving in won't be a shock to you. People say, "Live together to get a feel for the person's living style." It's all a hoax. You set yourself up for failure because you're living with someone you're not in love with. That means everything the other person does will annoy you to no end. The socks on the floor, the tampon floating in the toilet, the urine on the toilet seat, the dirty underwear, and the plates and cups left where they were used will all drive you insane. Why? Because you're not in love with the person you're living with. This will postpone and may even cancel the wedding plans. On the other hand, if you focus on dating, courting, and falling in love with each other, when you get married and move in together, the small things won't bother you because you'll truly be in love. Truthfully, I didn't think like this when I was dating. I've been fortunate enough to make it to the other side, and hindsight is always 20/20. That's why I hope I can save you some heartache.

I know you think that by doing it the right way, it's going to drastically shrink your dating pool. You may be right about that, but quality is much more important than quantity. If you take the narrow road in this day and age, it may actually increase your dating pool. The reason is that you become rare, unique, and different. Everyone you meet will look at you like you're from another planet, and they'll be so intrigued. Honestly, that's what drew me to my wife. She was so different from any other woman I'd dated. She didn't jump into bed with me when I wanted to jump into bed with her. I couldn't go into her house and visit. She made me stand or sit outside and talk to her until we became a couple. Her poise and presence were calm and confident. She wasn't into debating, baiting, or arguing like the other women I'd dated. I was intrigued, and that made me want to get to know her better.

Don't be afraid to do things differently and to value yourself like no one else does. It can pay off for you, and if it doesn't make a relationship work, at least you'll know you didn't lose yourself in the process. Don't be afraid of doing the work. I'm watching people do the work and get the reward. Yes, it's happening every day. Virgins and born-again virgins who've made the mistake of having premarital sex but have turned over a new leaf are abstaining until marriage. You can't knock it until you've tried it. Don't operate from fear. Operate from self-love and self-respect.

ENGAGEMENT

Engagement should look a lot like dating. This should come between twelve and twenty-four months of beginning a relationship with someone. If the man is serious about the woman, he will not wait five, ten, or fifteen years to ask for her hand in marriage. It's just a fact. I know some men make it look real by getting a woman pregnant, buying a house together, and all that, but if he doesn't ask for her hand in marriage, it's not real. I hate to break it to you like this. It's not real. He's still unsure and waiting on an opportunity that will make leaving her worth it. It's not that he doesn't believe in marriage; it's that he fears marriage. He fears the commitment of marriage. In his mind, marriage means he can sleep with only one woman for the rest of his life, and he's not ready for that yet. He may not be cheating on the woman, but he's not in love with her and he doesn't know if she's the one with whom he wants to spend the rest of his life. Men in this situation won't admit to this truth publicly in a million years. It would go against the "guy code" and upend everything he's worked for. Men have admitted this to me in private, even though I didn't need them to because I'm a man and I know the root of the choice not to marry.

The engagement will come around the twelve-month mark if the man truly is into the woman. It will definitely come before the twenty-fourth month if it's real. The engagement should last a year, just as stated in the Bible. A twelve-month engagement allows both parties to see if marriage is truly what they want. It's not a time to move in together and start having sex. The engagement is not a test drive. It's not a time to explore each other sexually and so on. That's what marriage is for, and you'll have the rest of your lives to continue exploring, building, and bonding. Keep the engagement sacred, and use it for its true purpose. Shift your mind-set to marriage, and court and converse with a marriage mind. The engagement should be a time for making a deeper connection, spending more time together, and having deeper conversations, but without having sex and living together. This will allow you to make love to the mind instead of the body. I'll talk about that in a later chapter. The engagement will feel like marriage because to be engaged is a commitment to marry. In your mind, it's like being locked into a contract to marry the person, but the benefits of marriage are not there yet.

If you are both over the age of twenty-five, the engagement shouldn't be longer than twelve months. Get married, or move on with your lives. If it's real, it's real, and when you know, you know.

MARRIAGE

If you haven't read my book *Make It Work*, please make sure you read it in its entirety after you finish this one. If you've read it, please read it again, and then read this one again. Get it into your spirit.

Marriage should happen within three years of beginning a relationship with a person. I believe it's the man's job to propose— not the woman's. Because of how a man is wired, I think a woman should never propose to a man—ever. It disrupts the natural order in a man's mind and starts the marriage off upside down and backward. You may never recover from a situation like that. Some women have told me I'm wrong, but that's because they don't know the man they've married. Time will tell, and they'll come back to me to discuss it.

A man who is ready for marriage will marry a woman within three years. Going to the county clerk's office or the justice of the peace is an option, and truthfully, it's what I recommend. Too many couples start their marriage upside down with the debt of a wedding. My wife and I got married in the courthouse, and we are celebrating our thirteenth year of a happy marriage this year. The wedding doesn't matter; the marriage does. If you can afford a wedding without going into debt, by all means, live it up.

Ladies, the size of the ring doesn't matter. It's not a measure of a man's love. As a celebrity life coach, I can tell you that in most cases, the bigger the ring, the smaller the love. That's not always the case, but the size of the ring has nothing to do with love. It has everything to do with how much money he has or how he spends his money. Is he faithful? That's what matters! Does he know and love God? That's what matters. Right now, my wife has a unique and cute setup on her ring finger, and we love it. It's four white gold wedding bands and a Cartier love ring. Maybe someday I'll get her a three-carat diamond ring and get insurance on it, but until then, I'll focus on loving her to the best of my ability and continuing to be completely faithful to her in mind, body, and spirit. A lot of women today are single and passing up on good men because their focus is on the wrong things. We live in a society of comparison and competition. You want to spend someone else's money and live someone else's life. A woman gets a small diamond, and she's ready to cry and break up with the guy. It's better to wear a ring from a gumball machine and have real love than to have twenty carats on your finger and get cheated on. Trust me when I tell you. I see it every day. I saw a man buy his woman a ring that cost $1.5 million, and the relationship didn't last five years. They never even made it to marriage. Trust me when I tell you! Focus on the love—not the wedding, the house, or the size of the ring.

Sheri's Perspective

I feel so bad when I hear the horror stories women are experiencing in relationships. I constantly tell people, I don't know if I would even want to date now if I was single. A lot of the reason I think women are settling in relationships is that there is a sense of desperation. With social media, it looks as if everyone is in a perfect relationship, having perfect babies, and living perfect lives. I can guarantee that in more cases than not, these "perfect" relationships are far from perfect, so trust me when I say you're aren't missing out on much. I know there is an innate desire to want companionship, but you also have to weigh the cost. It's better to wait for "Mr. Right" than "Mr. Right Now."

I didn't necessarily know the rules of engagement when dating, and though I definitely didn't do things 100 percent the right way, I would have had an easier road if I had done so. The first thing I did do before seriously dating was understand my worth. I never dated a ton in in high school because my mom was really strict, so dating for me wasn't really dating because I wasn't allowed to go anywhere with guys. Though most of the other kids started having sex in high school, I knew that wasn't the route for me. I valued my body more than that, and I also learned how to say "no" and avoid situations that would make me uncomfortable. I wasn't always the most popular because I was quiet, and I was okay with being alone if I needed to be. A part of truly valuing yourself is learning how to be happy alone. If you can find happiness being alone, you will never devalue yourself by being in a toxic relationship just for the need to have someone.

This relates to so many facets of life. Funny enough, my husband and I talk about this even now for ourselves and in the case of our son. My son was recently on a soccer trip, and although he is friends with everyone, he also is totally okay being alone and has chosen to do so more than once. Sometimes we will question him, like "Don't you want to go sit with your team?" and he always seems unbothered and fine where he is. I saw it really come into play on one of our travel trips. All the kids were hanging out in one of their rooms together, playing video games, and I told him to text me and let me know where he would be if they decided to change rooms. In about ten or fifteen minutes, I got a message from him, saying he was leaving the room. I asked him if everything was okay. He said yeah, but some of the boys were cursing and talking about inappropriate things and he didn't feel comfortable, so he and two other guys had decided to leave. I was completely blown away by that. How many sixth-grade boys would do that? So many adults don't even do that. There are two takeaways from that. One is that he has mastered the art of valuing himself. He values himself so much that he refuses to put himself into a situation that makes him uncomfortable. Secondly, he is okay with being alone. He said he had told a couple of the guys who weren't engaging in the behavior that he was going to leave and they had joined him, but even if they hadn't he was going to leave anyway.

If you can take those same principles into your relationship, it'll eliminate a lot of toxic relationships and all of the pain associated with them. Before entering a relationship, be okay being alone. Learn to find contentment and happiness while being alone. Fall in love with yourself, and learn your true value. Set standards (not preferences) that truly matter in a relationship. Pay attention to red flags, and never enter a relationship out of desperation. If you decide to enter a relationship, be okay leaving an uncomfortable or toxic situation. When you know what you are worth and what you deserve, you tend to attract the type of partner who can appreciate that and are okay with being better than the rest to be with you. It may take longer than it will for the next person, but the end result will be far better.

KEY TAKEAWAYS

+ It's better to wait for "Mr. Right" than settle for "Mr. Right Now."
+ Understand your worth, and value your body.
+ Learn to be happy alone.
+ Pay attention to red flags; don't ignore them.
+ Leave any situation that is toxic or makes you feel uncomfortable.

Chapter 10

LET HIM LOVE YOU

I've learned something from my wife that she probably doesn't know about and probably wouldn't agree with: she's never outloved me. That's my opinion. I say stuff about it sometimes, and then she runs off a list of stuff she does for me. Those are my petty moments that I have about once a month. You should never keep score in love, but it's human nature to sit down and count up everything you're doing for your partner sometimes. It's a bad habit, and we all have to get beyond it.

My wife will do anything I ask her to do, as long as it's not something crazy. What I mean by that is, anything I need done, she will take care of it. She actually takes pride in it. She works with me in our companies, and she handles a lot. I call her "The Closer." She's good at anything her hands touch. One thing I've learned from my wife is how to receive. She is not the type to turn down anything. On the other hand, I get upset if she buys me something without asking me first. The same is not true for her; if I buy it, she assumes we can afford it, and she gladly accepts it. I've gone broke in years past buying her gifts on a holiday. I don't spare any expense when it comes to her. Something in me makes me do it. If she has to wear clothes, I want her to have the best. If she has to have shoes, I want her to have the best. One day, I hope to give her the best wedding and the best ring. I'm away writing this book, and while she's home, I had a custom-made letterman jacket delivered to the house for her. On the left side of the chest, it says, THE CLOSER. It's black with a white outline. It's just her style. She loves wearing jackets because she's always cold. Just last week I was sitting there thinking what I could do for her because of how amazing she's been closing my speaking engagements and coaching clients. It's so much more efficient than when I was doing it myself. I love it. The crazy thing about the jacket is that after I'd ordered it, I was on the road for a speaking engagement and scrolling Instagram. I saw a picture of some amazing designer shoes. One was a pair of mules (I think they are called), and the pair next to it was designer tennis shoes. I have a guy who works at a fashion store in a mall, and I asked him if they had the shoes in stock. I'd already gotten my wife the mules awhile ago, but I loved the other designer shoes. I asked him if he could put a size eight to the side for her and I'd tell her to stop in and get them. She went to meet the guy at the mall and got the shoes. I got a text from her, and she absolutely loved them. I asked her how much they'd cost because I didn't know. She told me they were $700. After I caught my phone as it fell from the shock of the price, I smiled and replied, "Oh, great; not too bad." Then she said, "Oh, I thought you knew the price. You just sent me to pick up some shoes and didn't know the price?" No, I didn't know the price, and I didn't really care, to be honest. I knew the look on her face and the feeling in her heart would be priceless. That was what mattered to me.

There's something there: my wife allows me to love her, and she doesn't try to outdo me. Everyone knows that women are lovers and love comes naturally to them. It does not come as naturally for men. My wife tells me that some women admit that their men can afford to do nice things for them but don't. I can understand those men—barely—but I get it. It takes selflessness, and that's not easy for a human to do—especially a man. My wife has put a spell on me, I tell people. It's just her influence. It's hard to put into words why I want to love, give, and do so much for her. I see it as a God-like love. In Ephesians 5, the man is told to love his wife as Christ loved the church. As I think about the comparison that's drawn, Christ's love is unmerited. We don't deserve the sacrifice He made for us. We don't deserve the forgiveness, grace, and mercy He gives us. I take that into consideration when I love Sheri. It's not my job to love her at the level I think a woman deserves to be loved. It's my job to love her as Christ loves her. I want to give her more than she deserves and more than she thinks she deserves. Not just in gifts and things but in love, honesty, trust, and faithfulness. Just being 100 percent faithful to a woman is a lot of love, and it needs to be more common in our world. I give my wife a lot of gifts because it lights her up in a way nothing else does. She loves holidays, birthdays, birthday parties, and celebrations. And she loves gifts. They don't have to be expensive, either. I can give her a $10 Starbucks gift card, but it's the thought that matters most. I go to the mall and buy stuff about once a month, and the woman helping me will ask me, "What's the special occasion?" I tell her that it's a "for-nothing gift," and she always gets weak in the knees and grabs her heart. If it was a common thing, I know I wouldn't get that reaction.

If I buy my wife a gift from the wrong place in my heart or at the wrong time, I want her to say, "Babe, you don't have to do this, please take it back." But no, she doesn't say that; she accepts it with a huge smile, gives me a huge hug, and then wears it every chance she gets. I've learned from her response to be okay with being loved. My wife has taught me that it's okay to be loved and to accept love. It's a sign of a healthy self-image. A lot of women don't know how to accept love. If a man buys her a $100 gift, she goes and gets him a $200 gift. If he rubs her feet, she gives him a full-body massage. Women outlove men every day, and that is actually what has caused a lot of problems in our relationships. It's much harder for men to be loved and not get complacent. When a woman is loved the right way, it produces reciprocation. When a man is loved the right way, it produces complacency. We get accustomed to being catered to, and in return, we kick our feet up.

If I ask my wife for breakfast, she will make it. If I ask her for lunch, she will make it. If I ask her for dinner, she will make it. But please know that if I do not ask her, it is not coming. Yes, she's brought it before without me asking, but she does not make a habit of it. I actually don't want her to make a habit of it. It's important that a man loves a woman equally or greater than she loves him because of the nature of man. Truthfully, I think a man should love a woman more in order for the relationship to run as smoothly as possible. The reason is that men aren't natural lovers, so if a man doesn't love a woman more, the relationship most likely won't work. We are wired differently. Once a man falls in love, though, he begins to love in a way that comes naturally for a woman. Until then, the relationship always seems to be lacking an ingredient.

I've noticed that a high level of love and attention from a man is not normal in our society. If a man is in the mall with his woman and he's walking around with her, looking at clothes, those who pass by make comments about how sweet it is. It's not normal. To them, it's like seeing a cool animal at the zoo. A man at a nail salon with his woman is another rare sighting. I massage my wife's shoulders when we are out in public, and I can see women staring and starting to rotate their shoulders, trying to get their husbands' attention. They don't realize that I have a thing for physical touch and I'm always showing love in that way. If it's not my wife, then I'm playing in my sons' hair and massaging their scalp or squeezing their cheeks. But regardless of who it is I'm showing love to, other women will say something about it. It's what has helped me realize that as men we need to show love more and women need to learn to accept more love instead of always giving more.

There are some mental things that come into play in a relationship as well. As humans, we seek approval. We also reinforce behaviors that we want to see repeated. Early on in our relationship, I realized that my wife's energy changed so much when we went into a store to buy something. It could be a furniture store, a greeting card store, or any other kind of store. It was crazy to see how her energy would shift to a childlike energy on the night before Christmas. I love seeing that energy shift, so I want to reinforce it. It may stem from her childhood and not getting to shop much or get gifts much. She told me about her upbringing and how it was tough at times being raised by a mother who had come from Jamaica to raise her in the United States. Money doesn't grow on trees. She had help from her father and her aunt, but of course, they didn't give her money every day. She told me her family was evicted from apartments many times before she entered the ninth grade. That's a deep story. So being able to afford a new item from a store does something for her emotionally. I have picked up on that, and I realize that we all have our thing. It's important that as men, we recognize what it is that makes our women come alive and do it often. I've had guys tell me they broke up with their girlfriend or fiancée over her getting too excited about new bags, shoes, and clothes. Yes, it can be that way sometimes for men. Most men hate spending money on things for women because it's seen as frivolous. I had to learn that if Sheri likes it, I need to love it.

All men can get to the point of loving intentionally and unconditionally, but all women must get to the point of allowing it. Don't just give love; allow love. I don't recall the first time I heard someone say, "Allow love," but it's stuck with me ever since. It's much easier to give love than it is to allow someone to love you. We are so accustomed to being guarded that we rarely open up for love. It's time to open up to love. Let a man love you to the moon and back. If he buys you something, praises you, or changes the oil in your car, say, "Thank you" and let it be. You don't have to run out the next day and buy him something or try to outdo him in some way. Let the gift sink in. There is something powerful about being reinforced for giving a gift. We love the feeling of giving someone a gift and seeing him or her enjoy it. The smile on a person's face gives us a chemical release from our brains and fills our body with joy. Let the giver sit in that high and soak it all up. It's a natural high that can't be replaced. If women learn to allow love and let the man sit in that natural high, it will increase his love. If you kill his moment by trying to top his love, you send the wrong message. He will tell himself that there's no point in trying to love you better because you don't appreciate it, you always have to outshine him, and you're so much better at it than he is. He may stop trying.

Let him love you, and he may get close to your level of love. If he's not giving love, then give him what he gives you so he can see himself in the mirror. When he asks you why you're not loving him, you can tell him that you're giving him what he gives you because you thought that was what he wanted. Sometimes a man has to see himself in the mirror in order to change and do things differently. Most of the time, when a man doesn't love a woman right, instead of reciprocating at his level, the woman goes above and beyond, seeking his approval. He takes her love and still doesn't return it in equal or greater proportion, and that's when the relationship starts to become a burden instead of a blessing.

Women have to start commanding and accepting more love from men. You don't have to command it with words; you do it with actions. A man will read energy, body language, and efforts. He will sense that something is off, and he will go into Mr. Fix-It mode and start making tweaks to get things right. My wife has mastered this body language. I know when something is off, and our relationship is never out of alignment for more than twenty-four hours at a time. Every woman can do this, and it's not deceptive or manipulative; it's wisdom, self-love, and confidence. You have to know who you are and what you deserve. Understand what you bring to the table and what he needs to bring to the table to make the relationship work. It's not fair if you buy the groceries, cook the food, and wash the dishes. There has to be a balance in the relationship. The love should be mutual, and truthfully, the man should edge you out by just a little. You've heard the saying that you should let a man love you more than you love him. I believe it to be true because I'm living it. A man is supposed to cater to his woman and love her on a high level. She's a queen, and although she can reciprocate the love, he should lead in love and set the tone. It's not easy to accept the responsibility, but every man is capable of it. If he is required to do so, he can and will do it.

Sheri's Perspective

Tony always jokes that I love all five love languages and that he has learned how to be fluent in all of them. To be fair, it's the truth; I haven't met a love language I don't love. I had a tougher childhood than most. My mom was a single mom and at times had to work multiple jobs to make ends meet. I knew she loved me because of all the sacrifices she made, but she wasn't super affectionate. My dad I saw during the summer and holidays, but because we didn't really know each other, our relationship during my childhood was strained and I didn't receive much affection from him, either. It's important to spend time with yourself and determine the things that make you happy and be able to express those things to your partner. People can't read minds, and we shouldn't expect them to.

Because of some things I missed out in my childhood, birthdays and holidays are a big deal for me, and I made sure Tony knew that early in our relationship. We have a rule to never miss birthdays. He has turned down big speaking engagements to make sure he is here for my birthday or our sons' birthdays. Had I not expressed those things early in our relationship, he would have no idea how much these things mean to me. You can't have expectations and fail to communicate them.

Remember, you are deserving. Know your worth, and don't forget it. I believe both people in our relationship are equal. Tony knows that one of my love languages is gifts. He goes out of his way to buy random gifts just to show he appreciates me. It can be something really small, like a Starbucks gift card or flowers delivered when he is out of town. I appreciate the effort and never turn them down. A few times, I have told him he doesn't need to do that, and he actually got upset. He knows what makes me happy and does those things, and I have learned to enjoy them, appreciate them, and be thankful for them. I am deserving of these things, and I have to remind myself of that often. In the early stages of our marriage, I had a hard time accepting anything. I never asked Tony for anything, and if I couldn't afford something from my paycheck, I just wouldn't get it. As I have matured in marriage, I realize that we are teammates and we are one in our marriage. We aren't competing; we both try to operate from a place of selflessness and try to make the other person happy. When both people are operating from a place of selflessness, both are on the giving and receiving sides of love.

KEY TAKEAWAYS

✦ Let your man love you, and don't try to outdo him; a relationship is not a competition.

✦ Show the types of love you'd like to receive.

✦ You are deserving!

Chapter 11

WHEN WE PLAY MIND GAMES, EVERYONE LOSES

Woman are smarter than men in some ways. Men are smarter than women in other ways. When it comes to matters of the heart, especially relationships, women can be very dangerous if they want to be.

A woman's influence is lost if she plays mind games with her man. Men do not respond well to mind games, and the response will not be what a woman expects in the long run. Even though we men play our fair share of mind games, when a man is put into a position where he feels weak, confused, or lost, he can become vicious or violent. Things get out of hand quickly. It's an animal-like reflex to respond when we're backed into a corner.

There's a fine line between making strategic moves in a relationship and playing mind games. It depends on the purpose of the action. If what you're doing is to manipulate or deceive a man, it's a mind game. If what you're doing is to maintain your self-respect and dignity, it's not a mind game. We can confuse the two very easily. A lot of women ask me if the things I teach are mind games. No, they aren't. What I teach are rules of engagement. A mind game is rooted in deception or lies. There is no place for things like that in a relationship.

The problem with mind games is that they don't come from a genuine place. Anything that isn't pure can't have a positive return; it will always have a negative return. When you try to hurt someone else, you actually hurt yourself. Have you ever tried to hurt your partner and then realized that the game you're playing is actually hurting you more than it's hurting him or her?

You always have to ask yourself, "Where am I operating from?" If you're not operating from love, you're operating from the wrong place. If you're operating from anger, you become irrational and you're out for blood. Anger eats you alive on the inside, and it makes you want to hurt someone. Sometimes hurting someone could bring physical pain for which you will pay a great price. Holding on to anger makes you cut off your nose to get revenge against your face.

The decisions you make from a place of anger can have permanent consequences. That is why the Bible tells us to be slow to anger. It's very dangerous to allow yourself to be given to anger. I've seen women get angry and slice a man's tires, bust his windows, bleach his colored clothes, soak his phone in water, and the list goes on. The woman is angry, but she's not weighing the consequences of her actions. Instead of walking away from the relationship, she does something that will make it worse to be in the relationship. It hasn't dawned on her that he will never forgive her for what she's done, even though he pushed her to that point. She acted out of anger because she felt as if she had to get revenge or retaliation. Leaving the relationship wasn't an option because she doesn't know her worth.

Instead, she stooped to his level and tried to beat him at his game. Everyone lost. Now he's hurt beyond repair, and she's hurt beyond repair. That leaves two broken and hurting people who hate each other. How can a relationship last in these circumstances? It can't. The end is near. Mind games become toxic, and people are hurt every day because of retaliation and revenge.

I've coached so many women who have said to me, "I cheated on him because he cheated on me." That's a mind game. A man goes out and cheats because he's weak, insecure, and immature. There's an urge inside of him that's telling him he should cheat just for the sake of doing so. He hasn't learned enough, grown enough, or loved enough to be faithful, so he cheats. His girlfriend or wife finds out, and she's hurt beyond words. Then she decides she's going to make him feel the pain she's feeling. Her hope is that she can cheat, get caught, hurt him, and then they will forgive each other and live happily ever after. If she has to live with pain, he has to live with pain. She goes out and sleeps with another man. Building a full relationship with another man is out of the question. She needs a meaningless quickie just to prove a point and get some revenge. In her act of cheating, she contracts a sexually transmitted disease. Then she comes back to her man and has sex with him. Her boyfriend contracts the disease and finds out. By this time, he's trying to make things right with her, so he hasn't been cheating. There's only one place he could have contracted the disease, and that's from his girlfriend. He confronts her, and she confesses to it. She's crying, he's irate, and everything has hit the fan. Deep down, she hopes he will forgive her and stay with her because both of them have made bad decisions in the relationship. He excuses *his* cheating behavior and blames it on his nature and upbringing, but he holds *her* cheating behavior against her. Then he decides to end the relationship. The woman is lost and left alone. The disease is curable, but the damage done isn't. She's broken and doesn't feel fit to move on with another man. Her now ex-boyfriend moves on with his life and is in a new relationship within a couple months. Who won? Nobody. No one wins when we play mind games. Had she stood her ground and walked away from the relationship, she wouldn't have formed another soul tie with a new man, caught a disease, or lost her boyfriend, whom she actually loved. Walking away would have made him love her even more, respect her even more, and beg her to come back. When she came back, he would have worked for her love and grown as a man, and they might have had a chance at making it last forever. But because she stooped to his level, trying to beat him at his own game, he ended the games and walked out of her life. She lost herself and her relationship. He lost his relationship and goes into a new one a broken and bitter man, which means it won't be long before he tries to sabotage the new relationship, too. I know, because it's a true story. And there are more stories like it out there. Maybe you've lived through something like it.

Something that my wife has done to influence me is to never play mind games. What I see is what I get. I don't have to guess or wonder. Her actions are clear, and they are never about revenge. I'll write in a later chapter about her silence at times when she needs me to feel something. Even at those times, I know it's not a mind game because she's right in front of me and I'm very well aware of what I did or said that has upset her.

I've seen people instigate mind games because of past pain. A lot of us suffer from past pain. Have you been hurt in love before? If so, have you healed? Have you forgiven? Did everyone who came into your life after that relationship have to pay for the mistakes of your ex? If the answer is yes, then you know exactly what I'm talking about. If that's not the case for you, maybe you've been hurt by someone who was acting out because of their past pain. I've seen some men and women become detectives in their relationship. There's been no relationship crime committed, yet there's a star detective trying to solve a case that hasn't even happened. Men check phones and emails, too, but no one is better at it than a woman who has been cheated on in the past. Whereas she should have majored in forensics in college, she's wasting her skills in a relationship trying to find Blue's Clues on her man. She's calling family members, thinking they are code names for side chicks. She calls the local pizza place, thinking it's really a cover-up for a woman her man has on the side. Yes, there are men who have done things like that, but this man is innocent. She's trying to trap him in something he hasn't done, all because she's hurting. With every call, she's yelling at him and accusing him of cheating because he didn't call her while he was working. She texts him, and if he doesn't respond right away, she calls him every name in the book. Does he confess to cheating? No, because he's not cheating. What happens? One day, he calls her and tells her the relationship is over because he can't handle her insecurities and accusations all the time. She breaks down crying, and she can't breathe. It feels like the world is caving in on her, and she gets on the phone with me to talk through it. As she talks about the issue, she hears herself and realizes it's all her fault. She thought that if she played enough mind games with him, it would corner him into confessing that he was cheating. The catch is that he wasn't cheating. He hadn't even gotten comfortable enough with her to cheat on her. She busted the case before it happened. The case probably was never going to happen, but she caused another crime scene, and now he's gone. Yes, this happens every day. Past pain makes you act out of character. You do things and say things you shouldn't. If you don't heal before you deal, you'll end up playing mind games on yourself. No one wins.

You don't have to play games in a relationship. Be open. Be honest. Be trustworthy. If a man is trying to play you, it will eventually come to light because everything comes to light. Don't stoop to being sneaky, tricky, conniving, and manipulating. Keep your class, and let the rest handle itself. There's so much power in class and self-respect. When you operate with class, it makes a man want to get to know you better. He becomes so fascinated with your strength and poise that he doesn't have the time to deal with other women because he's too busy studying you. A lot of women don't realize that the best way to keep a man's attention is to be authentic and straightforward. There's no need to play games. The truth is stronger than fiction.

Mind games are a waste of time and energy. You lose the chance to truly love your spouse when you get trapped in mind games. The trust is lost because the relationship becomes more about competing against each other instead of winning together. I know you may read things online and in other books about playing mind games, but it's important to know what's a game and what isn't. If your intention is to deceive, manipulate, or control, it's a game. Don't give in to the games, and your relationship will benefit from the authentic bond that's built between you. Just be real, and everything else will handle itself.

Sheri's Perspective

Success in a relationship comes down to authenticity in many different forms. If you are playing games, you can push your significant other away. It's important to know how unhealthy mind games are for a relationship but also to know where they stem from. They go right back to confidence and self-worth. When you are confident in yourself, you spend less time worrying about what you think the other person is doing and focus more on you. Just trust that if something is going on, you will find out in due time. You also have to remind yourself that if the other person decides to do something like cheat, he or she doesn't deserve you and you don't have to play mind games to keep the relationship going. Love yourself enough to know what you deserve. Not only is it beneficial for your relationship, it is beneficial for your own mental space as well.

I have never been someone to check phones, emails, social media, none of that. I believe in the mantra "What is done in the dark will come to light." My husband coaches a lot of people on a daily basis; a large portion of them are women. I could be insecure, asking him questions, trying to listen to his conversations, but for what reason? If he is just doing his job and being faithful, my insecurity is going to push him away. Playing a mind game is a lose-lose situation, and in the process all you do is stress yourself out constantly playing detective, looking for clues every day.

Tony travels quite a bit and is usually in different cities speaking at seminars. A lot of women might feel insecure and think they need to go on tour with him or try to check up on him constantly. The seminars tend to run late, and then he and his team will usually go to dinner afterward. To be honest, some nights I am so tired that I can't even wait up to talk to him before bed. I send him a text saying "I love you, good night." Guess what? I sleep like a baby. I don't stay up half the night stressing or worrying. I don't have a reason not to trust him, and I am confident in myself. I remind myself that if he cheats or does something inappropriate, he would be losing something of value.

You may have to build the muscle to do this, and it may not happen right away. Different situations may make you feel uncomfortable, but you have to apply the principle "Fake it till you make it." That means that you fake being good at something until you actually are. When Tony started coaching a lot of celebrity women, I would start to question myself, compare myself to them, and even make up things in my mind. But immediately I would remind myself that I am his wife and I have no reason not to trust him. Even when I wanted to ask him questions or do things like check his phone or texts, I would fake the confidence I wasn't feeling until it eventually became my natural response. So, yes, in the very beginning, you might have to remind yourself every day of your worth, and that's okay. When you fake it until you make it for a while, you build that self-confident muscle, and it will change you and your relationship for the better.

One last reminder: There is nothing you can do either physically or emotionally to keep a person from cheating on you or leaving. Spending all of your time being insecure and playing mind games won't keep him and may end up pushing him away. Be confident in yourself and your relationship until proven otherwise. And remind yourself daily that you are worthy and it's his loss if he fails to realize that.

KEY TAKEAWAYS

+ If what you're doing is to manipulate or deceive, it's a mind game.
+ If you play mind games, you will both end up broken.
+ Don't retaliate or try to get revenge; don't cheat on him because he cheated on you.
+ If he decides to play mind games, he doesn't deserve you.

Chapter 12

COMPLACENCY IS THE ENEMY

Complacency in a relationship is when you stop doing the things you did to get your spouse. There is no traffic on the extra mile, and you stop going the extra mile. I'll admit that men are the first to get complacent. It's our nature to kick our feet up once we've got the girl. I was some kind of lover when I first got my wife. She reminds me about how I used to leave three-by-five cards with notes on them from the door to the bedroom, leading her to a gift. I would leave sticky notes in certain places I knew she would see them, just to remind her I loved her. I was a player back in the day, so I knew how to do everything right to get her hooked on my love. For me, complacency started to set in when my heart became pure and I wasn't trying to game her. Then I realized I couldn't become complacent just because I'd stopped playing games. I would have to find ways to keep the spark, even with pure intentions.

I've watched relationships fall apart over and over, and in a lot of cases, it's complacency that ruins everything. We get so familiar with each other that we stop trying to be sexy, smart, fun, loving, and caring. We start going with the flow, and we expect nothing to change. The fact that we're human remains. I coach it every week, and I see it play out every day. Women can recognize complacency, but it's hard to stop it from happening. Life happens.

Men are unique creatures. To call us superficial wouldn't be a lie. We are visual creatures by nature. We look at everything. We see everything. We look at men just as much as we look at women. There's an attraction we have to women, but still, we see everyone. Every man is visual, and we're always analyzing and people watching. The first thing a man notices about a woman is her looks. Then he scans everything else about her to see if he's attracted to her. The next thing is her energy and presence. Is she shy? Is she confident? Is she kind? Is she condescending? He's reading it all. Then he dives deeper into her personality to see if his personality can mesh with hers. Can she be a lover and also a best friend? These are the questions running through his mind.

Just like men, women present a representative. That means you show a man something that isn't real. You're nicer, sexier, and funnier than you usually are, and so on. All of your *t*'s are crossed, and all of the *i*'s are dotted. You're very aware of what signals you're sending. Everything seems to be perfect. Some women come in very strong. On the first or second date, the woman is hanging out at the man's place. Then she's cooking meals, cleaning up, and the list goes on. I've heard some wild stories of the treatment some men get in the courting phase. If you can imagine it, some women do it. I guess it's the desperation to be in a relationship. The man accepts it, but he will *expect* it—forever. It's not realistic, but he thinks it is.

Then the relationship is official. The man is won. First comes the marriage, then come the kids. In today's society sometimes, first come the kids, then comes the marriage. Whichever way it happens, it happens and you're off to the races to complacency. I've watched it happen when a woman has a child and she enjoys her pregnancy. The pregnancy fills her out in all the right places. Some women hate it, and they go on a crazy diet as soon as the baby is out. Other women are okay with it, and they take it easy. Then baby two happens. Sometimes baby three happens. Complacency, in a man's mind, is first determined by the woman's appearance. Does she stop wearing makeup? Does she stop getting dressed up? Does she work out? Does she sleep in her college sweatpants, or is she still looking for cute nightgowns that have a little sex appeal to them? Naturally, the relationship should evolve and you shouldn't have to put on an act for the rest of your life, but that's where problems arise. How much a woman did to get the man to fall in love with her determines how much she will have to do for him to stay in love. If you went to bed in hot pajamas in the beginning of the marriage and then, a few years in, you're dressed like a guy getting ready for an intramural game, problems may arise. Men are visual, so we expect things to stay pretty close to how we first found them—within reason. A grown man understands that every day isn't going to be a sexy day. A grown man understands that a woman's body changes and the more she gets comfortable, the more she relaxes, but we also still expect an effort to be made to appeal to our male senses.

Women may be okay with a man's potbelly acquired over time. Men, on the other hand, have some maturing to do in the physical appearance arena. Physical changes happen, but that doesn't mean he's happy about it. I remember a man saying to me once, "I married my wife when she was 115 pounds. Now she's 235 pounds. She's had two kids, and we both have put on some serious weight, but I just didn't expect this to happen." He was referring to her weight gain. Even though he'd put on 100-plus pounds, too, something in him felt that she should look better than he did. That was their complacency setting in. Both of them had been attracted to each other from day one. Their love is still there, but their bodies and sex appeal have changed. That complacency subtly affects the relationship. Then, when bodies change, sometimes attitudes change, too. Have you ever gone through a body change? It could have been weight, skin, hair, or anything. It affects you. It affects your self-esteem, confidence, and so on. If you don't feel sexy, you don't want to be sexy. Some things you can do something about; other things are out of your control. The key is to control what you can.

A woman loses her influence if she loses herself. If you don't control what you can, a man won't be interested in your influence in his life. But if he can see the love you have for yourself, he wants your love for his life as well. If it appears to him that you've given up and stopped trying, that's a hard blow for him. You have to pick your battles wisely. It's going to be a fight to try to keep everything together just as it was when you met your man, so choose your battles wisely. In twelve years of marriage, my wife still doesn't break wind around me. I truthfully really appreciate that. It's just something about a lady to me that says a woman shouldn't break wind publicly. She burps, and that doubles me over sometimes. I'm like, "Really, Sheri? Are you serious right now?" It's a double standard because I don't try to stop my bodily functions around her. I'm wrong for that, and I'm working on it. It's okay for us to keep our sexy around each other. Can you imagine how much better marriages would be if we actively cared about our sex appeal to our spouse?

My wife is something special. She still tries to prance around the house with a little walk when she knows I'm looking. As soon as our sons are around, she's strictly Mommy. All the sex appeal is out the window when our sons are around, but when they aren't, she does her best to look her best. I appreciate that she's not sitting on the couch breaking wind. She's not dressing like an intramural basketball player for bed. She's not letting herself go and throwing in the towel. There are hormone changes and things that women go through, and grown men understand that. It's the effort that counts. My wife spent $650 on face treatments this week. It was a sacrifice, but I respect it. She's going through something hormonal like women go through, and it's affecting her cheeks. She's never had any type of face breakout like this, but I've been told a woman's life can change in her thirties. It's minor to me but major to her. She could easily not care, but she does care, and I love that about her. The estheticians tell her that it's normal and women go through it at different times. I see it's tough on her at times, but I support her and tell her she's still beautiful and that I understand some women go through it from the age of thirteen. It's so cute to me to see her care so much about her appearance. It makes me appreciative because I've seen many people handle it totally differently. I've met couples who ended their relationships over complacency and the effects of it, and I've coached couples who were headed in that direction.

What are you doing right now? How close is it to what you did to get your spouse? My wife tells me she loves my body, but this isn't the body I had when I met her. Yes, I know I'm not supposed to look the same at thirty-five as I did at twenty-one. But guess what? There are thirty-five-year-old men who look like I did at twenty-one. What are they doing that I'm not doing? They are eating better than I am and working out more. If they can do it, so can I. If I had a medical issue, that would be totally different. I don't have a medical issue, so I can step it up. I don't eat anything by accident, so what I eat is a choice. If I'm drinking juice and soda, that's a choice. If I skip the gym for a month, that's a choice. I use myself as an example to say that complacency is a choice. If things happen beyond your control, it's not complacency—it's destiny. Please don't confuse the two. You have to do everything in your power to make sure you're not getting complacent. I don't know if my wife knows it, but I still try to look good for her. I did a little working out a month or so ago, and my arms started looking nice. So instead of wearing a T-shirt around the house like I normally do, I started wearing tank tops so I could get some extra looks from her. She says she likes my thighs and my butt. I remember asking my mom what she liked about my dad and she said, "His butt." That disgusted me, but that was her answer. Now I see this correlation between my mom's answer and my wife's actions. My wife has told me that some moms who have seen my older son playing have said things like "He has his dad's butt." I'm totally confused about why these types of comments are being made by women, but I'm beginning to learn that "men's butts matter." So I wear shorts that stop above the knee and they are a bit too snug in my opinion, but it's what's in right now.

My wife always says to me when I have them on, "I love to see you in shorts." I blush. I'm paying attention to what my wife likes and trying not to get complacent.

Evaluate yourself right now if you're in a relationship, or look back at your past relationship if you're in your single season. Do you know what complacency looks like in a relationship? You have to make an effort to keep your spouse physically attracted to you. Physical attraction matters, even when there's a deep love. It especially matters if you have some control over it. It's not that big of a deal if you can't control it. No one can blame you if you have an accident or go through something health-related. It's not your fault if things change under those circumstances. I can remember when I met my wife and would spend the night; I would sleep with a bandanna around my mouth. I told her that I didn't want any bugs crawling into my mouth. The truth was that I didn't want to slobber all over her pillow. On top of that, my stomach would be twisted up in knots trying not to let any gas go. I'd be about to pass out trying to hold in that gas. I was trying to be so sexy for her. I wanted to appear perfect. Of course, it's not realistic and I couldn't maintain that forever, but the effort still matters. She asks me now not to break wind in bed. She says she doesn't mind it other places, but she doesn't want me to break wind in bed. It can be annoying having a little something on your stomach and having to get out of bed and run to the bathroom just in case, but if it's going to keep the sexy going, hey, I'm with it. She told me that it's hard to feel sexy at night if I'm in bed passing gas. As I thought about it, it made perfect sense. This is a lighthearted example, but really think about it.

My wife still has an influence in my life because she's still the same person. I can tell she still cares about my feelings and my thoughts. Her respect and love for me haven't gone anywhere. The love she has for her body hasn't gone anywhere. She still goes to the gym and works out two to three times a week. I respect that, and I love that she's doing it. The metabolism slows down as we age, but I'm okay with that. Her body is doing what it needs to do. It's not where she wants it to be, but I absolutely love her curves. The fact that she wants to be in better shape says a lot to me. It lets me know she's not the type to get complacent.

That's the superficial side of things, but what about the things that go deeper? How is your attitude a year or two into the relationship? Do you talk to your spouse differently now that you're used to him? Do you curse at him? Is your tone condescending at times? Do you walk away when he's talking to you because you want to send a message to him? Check your attitude, and really ask yourself if you're giving him the same amount of attention and respect that you gave in the beginning when you both fell in love. I honestly feel that my wife gives me the same amount of attention and respect as she did when we first met. She still will talk to me until three or four in the morning, even though she has to wake up at 5:30. I try not to do it often, but it has happened a few times in the past year. It means a lot to me. We're still falling deeper in love, and that matters. Honestly, changing your attitude toward your spouse can be more damaging than letting your appearance go. Men expect women's bodies to change. We expect your hormones and skin to change. Wrinkles, lines, gray hairs—all of that is real. We expect it. But having a nasty and condescending attitude just because you know him like your shoe size—he wasn't expecting that change. I mentioned earlier that my wife saw a woman talking down to her husband and was blown away by it. I'd be willing to bet that the woman didn't talk to him like that when he was falling in love with her. Humans get complacent, but if you want your relationship to last and your influence to remain intact, you can't let complacency set in.

Don't get complacent emotionally. There can be several layers to this, but I'm focusing on sharing your emotions and always remembering the feeling of falling in love with your spouse. One thing I do is to stop and count everything I'm grateful for when I look at my wife. I think to myself about all of her amazing qualities and everything she brings to the table. That reminds me daily how special she is and that I'm very blessed to have her. When we get complacent, we start to see our spouse's greatness as average. The things he or she does exceptionally well become our norm, and we stop processing the emotions we felt when we first fell in love with those attributes.

Another side of the emotional complacency is when we stop expressing our love. Every month my wife and I find the time to look each other in the eyes and express our feelings. It's tough for me because it brings tears to my eyes, but it's a great practice because it keeps me emotionally connected. When you're emotionally connected in a relationship, you share real moments of love, concern, hopes, and dreams. It's important for your spouse to know that you're open to feeling deeply and showing those feelings in a positive and safe space.

It's also very important not to allow yourself to get spiritually complacent. When we get what we pray for, sometimes we stop connecting with God in prayer. That can affect your relationship in a negative way if you aren't spiritually grounded and don't hold true to your beliefs. Love can put you into a daze if you let it. You can lose your way because love seems to be the answer to all your prayers. Be mindful if spiritual complacency sets in and you're not praying like you once did. When you first meet a person, you may put a little extra sauce on your spirituality. We try to seem deep, spiritual, and really connected to God because we know it's attractive to a person who is looking for that in a spouse. Then, after the relationship has started, you can find yourself drifting. Make sure that you're focused and driven spiritually, because operating from a place of love, peace, and clarity will benefit your relationship.

Keep working not only in every area of the relationship but also in every area of your life. Make a list of the areas you need to focus on, and then write out things you can do to remain sharp in those areas. I set reminders on my phone to do things for my wife. I realize that work and meetings are scheduled. We will schedule everything but our relationship. In a lot of cases, what's not scheduled doesn't get done. I put my time with my wife on my calendar, and also other thoughtful things to do. I did this early in our marriage, when I realized my focus was becoming earning a living. I know that a lot of men struggle with work-life balance. I wasn't immune to that. I put everything on my calendar to make sure my life kept a balance. After doing it for a few months, it became second nature. It was like training wheels for me until I formed a lasting habit.

I know this can be a hard chapter to read if you've changed in a lot of ways, because life changing is hard. It's not anything to get down about; it's something to get up for. Take pride in growing and becoming a better person every day. Work on your attitude, spirit, and mind-set. Keep loving your body and taking care of yourself the way you're supposed to. It gets harder the older we get and life gets more demanding with work and family, but you have to prioritize you. You matter, and your relationship matters. Remember that love is a job you can't retire from. There is no finish line in this marathon. It takes work to love yourself, to love others, and to maintain a relationship. It is hard work, and the work won't do itself. If you don't want to do it for yourself, then keep growing for the one who wants to love you for the rest of your life. I don't know what my wife's motivation is, but I'm glad she's motivated because it's actually motivating me.

Sheri's Perspective

Self-worth and mutual respect are the themes of this book. In my opinion, those two things impact the success two people have in a relationship more than anything else. I know that talking about maintaining your physical appearance as a woman can be a controversial topic, but I'm a woman myself, so I'm allowed to talk about it, lol! This topic has two main parts. The first is loving yourself enough to keep up yourself. Of course, I want to be visually appealing to my husband, but I also keep myself up as well as possible because it makes *me* feel good. If you really love something, you take care of it. When someone buys a new car he or she is proud of, he or she washes it every week or more often and keeps the inside vacuumed and junk free. If you have kids, you take care of your kids because you love them. You make sure they have what they need, that they look nice going to school every day, and so on. Well, the same should go for you. If you love yourself, you should take care of yourself.

Everyone's self-care regimen is different, but we all should have one. When you spend time taking care of yourself, you feel better about yourself. You can be a wife, a parent, or a friend. You ever notice that when you get dressed up for a nice event, you feel like a princess and have a natural high all night long? That feeling can be daily in some form for you if you do little things to take care of yourself. We have only one life, so why not do small things every day to make yourself look and feel good and in turn keep your relationship fresh.

The other thing that I think about while making that effort to keep up with myself is the golden rule. How would I feel if my husband decided to no longer care for himself? Would I still be attracted to him if he were no longer making an effort? I want to look at my husband and be attracted to him, so I make sure to try to do the same for him. How would you feel if your significant other looked completely different than when you first met him if he no longer groomed himself the way they should or no longer got dressed and took pride in his appearance? Remind yourself to make small efforts to prevent this from happening on your end. Of course, as you get older, things change. You have less time to devote to the gym, you gain weight with pregnancies; don't try to hold yourself to an unrealistic standard, and don't beat yourself up about not being the same size you were in your twenties. It's about doing small things every day to make yourself feel and look good, which in turn strengthens your relationship.

Self-care helps you not only physically but mentally, and that alone is important. Everyone is different, but you need to figure out what the things are that will help you and implement them. Daily devotion definitely helps remind you of your worth, and it's also great for reminding yourself how much God loves you. I love to read, so getting lost in a book is a big part of my self-care. As an adult, it's hard to make time to read, but I have recently made it a priority because it makes me feel good. When you are doing things to maintain yourself and you feel good about yourself, you are more confident in your relationship. You are able to stand up for what you deserve, and you don't feel the need to play mind games out of insecurity.

KEY TAKEAWAYS

✦ Respect yourself enough to take care of yourself for you and your spouse.

✦ Men are visual creatures by nature.

✦ Don't get complacent; make sure you give the same energy you want to receive.

✦ Take time to figure out the things that are important to you, and make them a priority.

✦ Give each other the same amount of time and attention as you did when you were started dating.

Chapter 13

JUST SAY "NO"

The funniest thing to me is when women ask me how to tell their boyfriend or husband something they want to tell him. I'm always like, "Ummm . . . just tell him." I'm guessing that men are feared to some degree. Is your man violent or something? In most cases, the answer is no, he's not violent at all. Then why are you afraid to speak your mind to him? Yes, men can be fragile and we hate rejection, but we've been yelled and screamed at by coaches and teachers all our lives. So to hear a cool and calm "no" shouldn't be a problem.

I talk a lot with my wife. I'm always calling meetings, so she's never once had to sit me down to discuss an issue in our marriage. She knows she can just bring it up when I call a meeting. Doing what I do as a relationship coach, I know how things left unsaid can turn into a big problem one day, so I address the little things every month. At that time, my wife tells me what she needs to tell me. I can't ever recall her saying "We need to talk." I always beat her to it. We work through whatever the little issue is, and we move on. In these talks, she's no longer afraid to speak her mind. We've gotten to that point because I create a safe space for her to speak in and let her know that clear communication is the only way we can function. When I first met her, she wasn't a good communicator. When it was her turn to speak, her emotions would overtake her and she would shut down. I realized that it was because of my approach. As a twenty-three-year-old, I was more assertive and aggressive in my tone, which didn't create a safe environment for my wife to raise issues in. But as she found her voice in the relationship, it made things much better. I realize that I need to hear what I can do better, just as much as she needs to hear it. I'm always confused as to why so many women can't speak their minds in a cool, calm manner. I'm here to tell you, it's okay. You can tell your man "no." Just practice it. "No." Tell him what you're thinking, what you're feeling, and what you need from him.

My father would always say to me, "In a time of peace, prepare for war." You have to address things before they get out of hand. You have to call town hall meetings and get everything out onto the table. Then find a way to move forward, addressing the issues that have been raised. If you don't do that, you'll sweep everything under the rug, until one day you trip and fall over the mess you've ignored.

Men speak and think in straight lines. What we need to say and what we need to hear are direct communication. I'm sure you've heard a man say, "I can't read your mind." Yes, we get in our feelings at times when you're direct, but it's all about how you say things— not what you say. It helps a man if you speak in clear-cut sentences and are very direct. That's the only thing men respect. If you're afraid to speak, a man recognizes that and he can't take you seriously. As men, we are used to speaking directly to each other. The man who can be the most direct with other men is seen as the alpha male. A man who beats around the bush and doesn't say what he needs to say, he's run over. The guy beating around the bush may actually be physically stronger and tougher than the direct guy, but the direct guy wins the mental battle. Have you ever watched gangster movies and wondered what made one guy the most powerful and feared man in the city? It's not his size or muscle. It's his communication style. He's direct and blunt. He doesn't hold back any thoughts. His words can get him killed or get others killed. When I watch the movies, I ask myself, "Why doesn't someone just shoot him?" I'm curious how one man can get so far just by his communicating and everyone buys into his strength without him even having to flex any muscle. It's just his communication style. If a woman does the same thing with her man and can speak her mind respectfully, she can command the most respect from him. A man may literally become putty in her hands, just because of her communication. I watched a documentary about the drug queen Griselda Blanco. It was interesting to me how a woman entered a man's game and dominated. She had men selling drugs and killing other men for her. All she did was tell them what to do. If she wanted someone killed, she would tell another man to kill him. It was her confidence and communication style that made men fear her. She wasn't physically stronger, taller, or bigger than any of the men taking orders from her. Her presence and tone just made her seem so sure of herself that it convinced everyone around her to be sure of her, too. Although that's a negative example, the lesson still remains: by being sure of yourself and direct about your values, needs, and concerns, you can gain the respect of a man.

It's not magic; it's confidence. You've heard it said that dogs can sniff fear. I don't know if it's true for dogs, but it's true for men. Once we realize that a woman fears us, it's in our nature to dominate, even if that wasn't our initial intention. It's the warrior in a man that makes him control a situation when he feels he's the strongest in the room, not just physically but mentally as well. I can look at my wife and tell she doesn't fear me. She respects me, but she doesn't fear me. If I ask her a question, I get a straight answer. I don't have to read between the lines. It's very clear to me what I can and can't do in our relationship. She doesn't hold back her thoughts or feelings about what's acceptable and what's not. I've asked her if I could go to the club, the casino, and so on. I don't have a desire to go to any of those places, but I've asked her just to hear her response. She knows what it means for a man to go to those places and how the temptation can devour him. She looks at me and says, "Absolutely not," without even batting an eye. I believe her. She really means it. I've had the same conversation with other women, and their answer might be different. Some are just as sure as my wife, but others are like, "Well, I guess it's all right. I mean, you have to let a man be a man, right?" I'm on the other end of the phone like, "Absolutely not." If you let a man be a man, you won't have a man for long. You have to set boundaries and be very direct about what's out of bounds, or he will live out of bounds and the relationship will fall apart.

Confidence is the key. I watched my wife grow into herself. As she dealt with her past pain and got over the hurt and anger of her past, it changed her communication style. When we are angry and hurt, we explode when it's time to communicate. If we're cool, calm, and collected, we are able to speak directly, with ease and poise. As I watched the shift happen in my wife, I realized that I could respect her even more than I already did. You should never speak if you have to yell, curse, or cry while trying to express yourself. Wait until you've gathered yourself and can speak directly without any interruption from your emotions. Clear communication is respected. If it's not clear and unobstructed, it's not received properly. Men don't receive words delivered with tears. Tears break a man down and make him feel vulnerable. His "Mr. Fix-It" light comes on, and because he can't fix it, it angers him. His anger and confusion block his ears from hearing and his mind from processing. If you have to cry, wait a few days until you've cooled off and gathered yourself, and then say what you need to say.

Learn the word *no*. Can I go to the strip club? No. Can I go to the club? No. Can I go smoke weed with the boys? No. Can I go to Vegas to gamble? No. Can we have a threesome? No. Can I have a hall pass? No. Can I watch pornography? No. Can I stop going to church? No. Just as a child, a pet, a boss, a friend, and everyone else tries to get as much out of you as they can, your man will do the same thing. Just say "no." It's okay to say "no." Put it into your arsenal, and use it as you need to. It's not being controlling or overbearing if you say "no" to things that go against your morals and values. It's very important that you say "no" to those things. Otherwise, you're saying "yes" to the end of your relationship as you know it. Eventually you'll lose all control, and the things you allowed to happen that you knew shouldn't have been happening will cost you everything you've worked to build.

We want to hear "no." "No" is also a form of love. If the answer to everything is "yes," it causes a lot of problems. If a man can get away with anything, he has no reason to respect you. All influence is lost when you can't say "no."

You're not a teddy bear to be used in any way your man wants to use you. We put teddy bears through a lot. Yes, they get love, and some have cute outfits, but they also get all the pain, too. You're not a human teddy bear. Speak up for yourself, and demand respect. If it's against your will or you just don't feel like it, then say so. Do you recall your parents telling you "no" to certain things? You were angry in the moment, but as you got older, some of it made sense. You're actually thankful they said "no" sometimes, right? It's the same in a relationship. Your man may give you some attitude, but deep down, it builds respect in his heart for you. It shows him that you're a real woman and can stand up for yourself. You're not a sex slave. You're not a maid. You're not a butler. You're not a side chick or concubine. You're the queen of the castle, so act like it.

The more you're able to express your feelings in a time of peace and say "no" to the things you need to say "no" to, the more he will respect you. Eventually he will stop trying to test the limits and will stay in bounds without being told. All of the questionable stuff will be off the table, and you'll have a tamed and responsible man. Remember, you teach a man how to treat you by what you allow, what you stop, and what you reinforce. Just say "no"!

Expect some pushback in the beginning. The silent treatment may come. He may get some distance from you. It's all a test to smoke you out of the "house of no." If you surrender, you'll never get the respect you deserve. If your "no" is legit and justifiable and you're not just being rude and impossible to deal with, he will come around. If he doesn't respect "no," he doesn't respect you. It's important that you get to this realization as soon as possible. Don't waste ten years of your life only to find out that your man doesn't respect "no."

The constant "yes-woman" loses everything eventually. Why? It's human nature to take everything a person is willing to give. You will be out of love, money, home, and everything else you brought to the table. A man will chew you up, spit you out, and walk out of your life if you don't have "no" in your backbone. I've done it, and I've seen it happen to other women.

Women ask me all the time, "Why did he leave me for her after I was here for him all these years and did everything he ever asked of me?" The answer is in your question. He left you because he used you for everything he could get from you. He never met a "no," so there was no need for you any longer. He's settling down with the woman who has the heart to tell him "no." I'm with the only woman who told me "no," and I felt she meant it and it wasn't a mind game. I met her when I was twenty-one years old and immediately knew I had to turn in my player card. *This woman is different*, I told myself. I'm used to women saying "yes" to everything I ask them. This woman says "no." I love it. If I can run over her, I don't want her. If I can do anything I want to, I know I'll lead myself to destruction. Having a woman who has found her voice has made me a better man. Everyone wants someone who makes him or her better. Think about it. Even women want men who are sure of themselves and confident. If you can run over a man, you don't want him. You respect his "no" because it looks like confidence and strength to you. You like a man who isn't afraid to hold you accountable and push you to be better. Even his reassurance that says you're better than what you're settling for in your career is sexy to you. When he says, "No, you can't accept that, you're better than that," it makes you love him even more. The same thing goes for men. No one wants a weak, timid person who doesn't know his or her self-worth. We will pray for you and wish you the best, but we want some backbone. I hear women say all the time, "He's too soft." What does that even mean? It means he doesn't have "no" in his backbone.

Take it as a lesson, and find your voice. What are you allowing a man to get away with? What did you allow in the past that's still haunting you today? Do you have a voice? Do you know your voice? Are you afraid of your man? Do you fear being alone? Answer those questions again, and make sure you're not shrinking in your life. Be who and what you're called to be. There is power in your "NO."

Sheri's Perspective

Learning to say "no" and speaking up for yourself requires confidence, but it also requires you to be reasonable and realistic. Everyone likes structure and stability to some extent, whether they admit it or not. Our kids probably live a more structured life than any of their friends or most kids we know. We give a lot and expect a lot, but we also spend time with them, speaking into their lives and helping them grow. My older son doesn't watch TV or play video games during the week. And some weekends, if we are away for soccer, he doesn't even get the chance to do it then. The other day he said, "Mom, I am glad I don't play during the week, because if I did I would be rushing through my studying and work trying to get to play, and then I wouldn't be doing as well as I am." He realizes the benefit of the structure, and it's helping him thrive. Just like you don't let your kids do everything they want because you know the end consequences, that's the same way you have to be in your relationship. Human beings naturally want to be the best version of themselves, so we are drawn to people who bring that out of us. Have you ever noticed that a girl will be dating a man and he was a dog to her, and then she will watch him move on and become a better man for the next girl. That next girl knew the power of her voice and influence, and her confidence helped change the man. Until you have the confidence in yourself to say "no" and express your thoughts and feelings, you will see no growth in your partner or in your relationship.

The other part comes down to being reasonable and realistic. There is a big difference between learning to have a voice and saying "no" and being controlling and unrealistic. When you say "no," have a valid reason and genuinely have the best interest of your partner and relationship in mind. Some people say "no" out of insecurity or just to flex their control and power in the relationship. When you use your voice with the wrong heart, it will push the other person away. People can feel authenticity, and when you are coming from a place of love, they can feel that, too. Remember, your heart has to be in the right place and you have to operate from a place of self-confidence to effect change in your relationship in a positive way.

HOW TO SAY NO

The Tone of Your Voice Is Everything

Always speak out of love and be cool, calm, and collected. The other person will be more likely to receive what you are saying rather than getting angry and shutting down.

Be Reasonable, and Be Realistic

Make sure you are saying "no" to benefit your partner, not control him. Don't abuse your influence, because if you do, you may never have that influence again.

Be Confident in You

Saying "no" and speaking up for yourself or for your relationship require confidence. You have to know you deserve those standards and be okay requesting them from your other half.

Chapter 14

HONOR AND RESPECT

A woman's influence is lost if the honor and respect in the relationship are lost. There are many ways this can happen, and I've touched on them some already, but there's more. Social media are ruining relationships today, too. In the vulnerable stages of relationships, people are turning to social media to get their followers on their side in an effort to bash their partner. I've been guilty of posting something that speaks to a discussion I've just had in my relationship and then getting thousands of likes. It's abusive. That's a strong word, but I have to call it what it is. I'll call it social abuse. To take your business to the social media streets, share your side of the story, make it sound perfect and flawless, and then let the likes and comments pile up against your partner is disrespectful, and it hurts the relationship.

My wife told me early in our marriage that that's one thing she hates. I heard her, and I never did it again. She spoke her mind, and I felt it. It was tough for me, because I had built my brand on authentic quotes from the heart. I had to learn that there are boundaries. My wife is such a woman; she never did that to me on social media. Well, she's posted a couple of quotes that I felt stepped on my toes. I asked her about it, and she had a quick response that made me feel like I was reaching. In fact, I was reaching. Her post had nothing to do with our relationship. It's crazy how social media can be used in a disrespectful and dishonorable way toward your partner. It's also interesting how we can misread social media, take things out of context, and apply them to our relationship.

In the comments section of my posts, I see women tag their boyfriends and husbands. My post is something that would step on a man's toes if he were walking out of line. In the comments, the woman tags the boyfriend and says, "You need to follow him." What she's really saying is "You need to take advice from Tony Gaskins because you messed up and he'll set you straight." I cringe when I see it, because I'm a man and I know how snatching a man's chain triggers him. It's painful and humiliating, and a man doesn't bounce back from it well. I've seen women grandstand on their men online in my comments section. Some men lash out publicly and curse the woman out right in the comments. It's painful to read. That type of behavior removes all honor and respect from the relationship.

How hard would it be to screenshot my post and text it to her boyfriend? Or sit beside him and show him on a phone? But instead she tags him so all of her friends and family who follow me can see that she called him out. She thinks she's getting some clout and respect from my followers. Truthfully, she's about to get kicked out of his life.

Social media is becoming very toxic for relationships. There's so much harm that can be done online. A woman tags a man in all the posts she wants him to see. Then the man likes all the pictures of half-naked women that he can find. They go back and forth, stripping their relationship of every bit of respect it has left. Before they know it, they're at each other's throats and wondering how they got to that place. Honor and respect are a two-way street. If you don't give it, you won't get it.

Have you ever heard the saying "Praise in public, criticize in private"? I heard it before I met my wife, and I've never forgotten it. When you criticize your partner in public, you're operating from the wrong place. You're purposely trying to humiliate him in front of everyone, thinking the public humiliation will drive your point home even better. You have actually just started a fight that will be carried on when you get home. Sometimes it's small things we don't even think about. I remember having a couples game night at our house once. There were about five couples at our house to play games. My wife chose the games from Pinterest, and she got all the materials we needed and set everything up. There was a certain way you were supposed to play the games, but some of it didn't make sense to me. I felt like she was taking the long route and adding unnecessary steps to the game. I walked up to her and whoever it was getting ready to play the game and asked, "Hey, why don't you do it like this?" That upset her. I think it maybe was my second or third time suggesting a different way. She kind of mumbled to me, "Why do you keep doing that? I don't tell you how to do stuff." I didn't know she was taking her job so seriously. I thought she'd laugh and say, "Oh, yeah, you're right, that doesn't make sense." I forgot how competitive she is when it comes to games. She was in game mode, and I was interrupting her focus. I also had some valid points, and it made her look like she didn't know what she was doing. It embarrassed her. That wasn't my intention, but that was what happened. I don't get to choose how something I say or do makes her feel. Even if I feel she's being overly sensitive, I have to respect her feelings. That's honor and respect. I share that to show how even something you see as small could be a big deal to your spouse. Once you learn what honor and respect mean to him or her, it's your job to do that.

I can't think of a time my wife has actually embarrassed me in front of people. I guess because she knows how it feels, she's very mindful of how she speaks to me in public. I seem to be the one always saying the wrong thing. If I said something she didn't like, she would make a face. Then I'd tell her to fix her face because people could be watching us. I didn't realize that the fault was mine and if I had thought before speaking, she wouldn't have made a face. She's never been the type to hide an emotion. Pretty much, what she's thinking shows on her face. I had some early lessons on relationship-in-public etiquette.

Once honor and respect are gone, it's hard to get them back. It's important to sit down with your spouse and talk about what they look like to you. Express how you want to be spoken to and treated. Then listen to how your spouse wants to be spoken to and treated. Once the ground rules have been laid, you have to stick to them. This helps the relationship flourish. Don't get into the habit of going tit for tat. If you feel you were disrespected, instead of retaliating, let it go in public and then address it in private. We don't often think like that. I have to check myself and realize that I'm operating from the wrong place when I choose to address something in public. It may not be in a way that others can hear what I'm saying, but they can see the expression on Sheri's face if they're looking. Her reaction to what I'm saying might be dramatic, with the intention of someone seeing it, knowing it would embarrass me. That's tit for tat. We can both say we didn't mean it or it wasn't our intention, but it's better to be safe than sorry and not do it at all.

Another form of disrespect is gossiping about your relationship. How many times have you said something negative about your spouse to a friend or family member? It always comes back in some way. Typically, the person you told comes around and shows his or her disdain for your spouse with awkward energy. Typically, this happens in young relationships. My wife used to tell her friends and her parents all of our business. The reason she did it was to gain their love and protection instead of their resentment. She broke the rules of her upbringing by getting married and pregnant before graduating college. That confused her friends and angered her parents. Had she ridden into the sunset with me and never looked back, she might have alienated them. I wasn't doing everything right, so her going to her family for vent sessions brought out their love for Sheri. The issue was that the friends and family looked at me like the bad guy. I returned the favor and did the same thing to her by talking about her to my family. We were in our early twenties, so those mistakes were to be expected, but we didn't fully understand the repercussions of them. For a while, her family hated me and my family hated her. We dishonored our marriage by going outside the home with petty remarks about each other. Then came the tall order of trying to undo what we'd done. We shifted into a place of honor and respect, and that was when things started to change for us. My wife had to undo the damage she'd done with her friends and family, and I had to do the same with mine. Here is the way that looks: You stop reporting the petty news, and you start reporting the good news. You deal with your issues in-house and then take the positive results to your friends and family. When you're talking to others, tell them all the good things your spouse does for you. At first, they won't want to hear it, but the more they hear it, the more their hearts will start to change. In addition, you have to report good things about your friends and family to your spouse. Tell your spouse about the nice things your friends and family said about him or her. On your spouse's birthday, tell him or her that your mom, friend, or whoever said "Happy birthday." Keep piling it on little by little, and eventually the other person's heart will start to heal and forgive. Now I'm the perfect husband in the eyes of my wife's friends and family. They've seen my growth and maturity over the years. The same goes for my friends and family. They see my wife differently now because I changed the narrative. Don't ever isolate yourself or suffer abuse in the name of love, but also don't exaggerate the bad and minimize the good just to get attention. It's not fair to have your spouse working for your love and your friends and family working for your love, while the two sides are against each other. That's deception, and it will bite you in the butt.

Honor and respect aren't just a public thing. They're even more important in private. I remember that a man told me his woman said to him, "You'll never succeed in life." He eventually divorced her, but he never forgot what she said. Even after all of the wrong he had done to her, he held that one comment against her. She'd said that to him in a one-on-one conversation. You'd think that's where you're supposed to say it, but if it's toxic, there's no room for it even if that's truly how you feel. To dishonor your relationship in private is to destroy it in public. You're stripping away at the fabric of your love, and soon you'll be left with nothing. Criticism is rarely constructive, so you have to learn how to word it. Instead of pointing out everything you think your spouse does wrong, point out the things you'd like him or her to do. It's the same thing, just worded differently. Don't get caught up in your feelings and allow your anger to make you disrespect the one you claim to love. Protect your love, and protect your spouse. We all make mistakes, but they can be fixed. It takes time and real effort to fix them, but if you're committed to the work, it can be done.

You may have a friend or family member who hates your spouse for no other reason than your spouse took his or her place. Your friend may try to talk bad about your spouse to you and plant seeds of negativity. You have to stop that in its tracks and turn it around. Let your friend know it's unacceptable and that you will cut him or her off if he or she keeps it up. You know what he or she is saying is not the truth, and it's coming from jealousy. Your friend may not be able to accept the fact that your relationship comes first now, and he or she may want to try to ruin what you're building. Honor and respect are also checking people without your spouse knowing what you're doing. If you bring all the bad stuff you had to shut down back to your spouse, you're instigating and making the situation worse. You have to shut it down and realize that you can handle it and your spouse never has to know what was said about him or her. That's honor and respect. You're fighting battles on your spouse's behalf and not asking for credit or praise for it. I know we can be petty and want to get praise for things like that. It's the wrong place from which to operate. You're trying to get kudos from your partner for sticking up for him or her, but what you don't realize is you're making your partner hate the friend you're setting straight. Don't play the middle against both ends anymore. Diffuse the hate and jealousy, and keep your hands clean. Your relationship will be better for these efforts. You may not realize it right away, but it'll make sense soon enough.

If you lose your spouse's respect, you've lost him or her. Protect it with everything in you. Don't let your pride or ego get into the way of your relationship. No one cares about your relationship but the two of you. If you allow anything or anyone to creep in, it will be destroyed. Don't expect people to be happy for you and want to save your relationship. There may be a couple of friends or family members who want to see your relationship succeed, but if you put your destiny into the hands of the outside world, you will be sadly mistaken. The world will destroy what you're trying to build. Dishonoring your spouse to get social clout or to make yourself feel better is never the way to go. Check yourself. Leave your pain, anger, and bitterness at the door, and don't let them into your relationship. Keep your words and actions above board, and you'll be thankful in the long run that you did so. You won't get too many chances at real honor and respect. You may make mistakes, but if you continue making them, they will cost you the love of your life. Do you honor and respect your spouse? Get to the truth of the matter, and it'll save your relationship!

Sheri's Perspective

One of the biggest issues we had early in our relationship was sharing every little thing with our families, sharing more bad news than good news and really just being petty. Granted, we were really young and immature, so that had a lot to do with it. But I see a lot of older people engaging in that behavior as well. The old saying "Treat your relationship like a house with the doors and windows locked" still rings true today. Of course, I am not referring to anyone experiencing abuse in a relationship. If that is you, by all means keep your family informed for your own safety. What I am referring to is the petty arguments every couple has, especially as you are figuring each other out in a relationship. Instead of communicating everything to everyone else, communicate with each other and figure out what works for you. Make rules for communication that work for you both as a couple, and stick to them.

As soon as we eliminated seeking outside opinions and attention from our families, our relationship made a turn for the better. We developed systems that worked for us and rebuilt our relationships with our families. In the process, you learn to stop focusing on small things and look at the big picture. When you focus only on the real issues instead of small petty ones, you realize you have so much more to be thankful for and way less to complain about. As you find the positives in your relationship, you have to share those things with your family and friends so they can see that your relationship is doing well and that what you were going through in the beginning was just relationship growing pains.

KEY TAKEAWAYS

✦ Listen to what respect and honor mean to your partner.

✦ Don't share meaningless negative things with family and friends.

✦ Learn to work through your problems in-house.

Chapter 15

TRUST AND FREEDOM

Recently, I was told about a situation where a woman met an amazing man. She said he was a ten out of ten on the looks scale. His annual income was over six figures. He worked out almost every day. The last relationship he had been in was over and done with completely. He was ready for something new and something real. The woman who got the opportunity to date him wasn't bad looking herself. She was also a ten out of ten in the looks department. She was a professional woman with a great-paying career, just like the guy. The situation she was coming out of wasn't far removed from his. There was some scarring left on her heart. They decided to give it a shot, and the man was up for the challenge of helping the woman heal. Every week, they went on dates and spent a lot of time together. The sex wasn't too far behind, and they hopped into bed to fulfill some lust. Things were going well, according to the dating times we're in today. The guy worked a pretty demanding job, so his phone time was limited. Still, he always called and never missed a day of contact. Sometimes it would be in the morning. Other times it would be at night, but he wouldn't let a day go by without reaching out to the woman to converse.

The guy was a major catch in the woman's eyes, and some panic started to set in. If he texted her in the morning and then didn't text again until after work, she'd flip out. He would check his voice mail, and there she was, three or four times throughout the day. They'd get on the phone, and she'd yell at him and interrogate him as if he had committed a crime. She was making all kinds of accusations, and the man just didn't know where the energy was coming from. Yes, she was successful, fit, and pretty, but something was off. They had been dating only a few months, but he felt like he was on the hot seat every other day. She thought there was no way he could be faithful if he didn't contact her all throughout the day. He worked in the field, so he would be en route from site to site, but she thought he could have called her in between jobs. Sometimes he would, and other times he wouldn't. The interrogations continued, and each time, she turned it up a notch. Then one day after work, he called her and told her that he wouldn't be able to continue the relationship because she was too insecure and jealous for no reason. He'd given her no reason to act the way she was acting. He'd flaunted her around town, at social gatherings, on walks in the park, working out together, and everywhere else one could imagine. Still, none of that was enough. She needed to know his every move, all day long. The breakup broke her, and she couldn't take it. There is a lesson in this. The lesson is that in a relationship, trust is a nonnegotiable. You have to give trust while, at the same time, making the other person earn it. The trust is there until it's taken for granted. It still has to be earned, but you can't take it away for no reason. The woman lost a decent man who could have turned out to be a great man. I see these true stories play out every day. Maybe you've lived through one.

I admit, trust doesn't come easy. Why don't you trust? Some people don't trust because they've been hurt in the past. After being hurt, it's hard to believe that someone else won't do the same thing. You're afraid and operating from a place of fear to the point that you attract the very thing you fear. The person you're with hasn't done anything for you not to trust him or her, but you're hurting from the past, so you hand out two strikes and he or she hasn't even gotten up to the plate to take a swing. That's the problem with pain: the past relationship sabotages your present one. Once you've ruined it, the opportunity may be gone for good.

There are some people who don't trust because they don't feel worthy of love. They assume that no one will be faithful to them because they aren't worth a commitment. Those self-defeating thoughts may stem from childhood or some trauma they've experienced. That causes them to lash out at someone they're trying to love just because of what's going on in their own mind. Insecurity is never a good look on you, and it pushes people away, when truthfully, you need them in your life.

Then there are those people who have done so much dirt, they fear that what goes around will come back around for them. They know that we reap what we sow, and they're waiting on their dish to be served. If you've ever been a cheater or a liar, you know exactly what the opportunity to cheat or lie looks like. When your partner is presented with that opportunity, you assume he or she will do the same thing you once did. That causes you to jump down his or her throat, accusing him or her of things that haven't even crossed his or her mind. It's your guilty conscience. That causes a lot of problems in relationships, and it keeps people in a constant state of anxiety.

Another problem is that people who believe things are too good to be true are probably right. If there are no problems in the relationship and everything is going smoothly, they seek to cause problems because they fear something bad is coming and they'd rather make it happen than wait for it to happen. They sabotage the relationship. *Everything is cool, so you must be cheating on me. There's no way you're not cheating on me. It's too good. Love isn't supposed to be this easy. Where's the text from random numbers? Why aren't men texting your phone? How have you been able to avoid being caught with someone else?* All of these thoughts run through their mind, so they concoct stories and false narratives, and then speak them out loud. It's very annoying to the person being accused, and he or she just can't figure out where it's coming from or what caused it.

One thing that has wrapped me up in my wife's love is her emotional intelligence and self-confidence. She has her struggles when she looks in the mirror, but she doesn't take them out on me. When I'm traveling and she's back home with our sons, she sends me pictures of her and the boys and tells me what they are doing throughout the day. I check my phone, and she will have sent me some updates on what's going on back home. In my line of work, I'm used to answering women's questions that stem from insecurity. I get on the phone with my wife, and there is not one question arising from insecurity. I know from the women I coach that some of them would be concerned that their husband, traveling alone, might be cheating. Not Sheri. It blows me away, and it makes me fall deeper in love with her. I want to eat out of her hand, hop online, and order her a "for nothing" gift or just do something crazy to say "thank you." It's so amazing to be in a situation that some might consider tempting, but her confidence is so radiant that it empowers me to work even harder for my family.

That trust strengthens the relationship, and it inspires me to trust her equally. The Devil tries to whisper in my ear sometimes, and I wonder how she can be so calm and confident when cheating is so common among men today. Then I slap myself back to reality, and I realize how much she loves our sons and me and that she'd never jeopardize that. I have to overcome my own insecurity because I was once a grown boy who didn't believe people could be faithful. My wife's confidence in me adds to her influence in my life. She can get more love out of me because of her calm demeanor. It's in this relationship that I learned a relationship should feel like freedom—not captivity. When I was younger, I was so accustomed to seeing relationships that looked like prison sentences that I thought that was how they were supposed to be.

Many couples are attached at the hip, and the relationship becomes so codependent that it's dangerous. It became normal to see couples acting like Siamese twins. But that's not how it's supposed to be. You should be in love and be best friends, but you should also be able to have your own life. Freedom doesn't mean freedom to sleep around and step outside the relationship. This freedom I'm speaking of means you can take a girls' trip or guys' trip and build with your friends without your spouse blowing up your phone all day. When I'm gone, my wife doesn't FaceTime me and try to hold me on the phone. She lets me focus and work, and I feel free and empowered. We speak when we can speak, and a lot of times, she falls asleep before I make it back to the room to say good night. That's peace and love. I'll read a text from her that says, "Hey, I'm so sleepy. I'll try to wait up, but if you can't reach me, I'm asleep." Of course, the Devil tries to whisper to me, "Oh, she's not sleep; she's on the phone with another man." But the Lord shows me the playback of how she falls asleep before her head hits the pillow every night. I'll literally be talking to her and look over, and she's sound asleep. We lie down for bed and I think we are going to watch a little television together, and literally, in less than five minutes, she's asleep. Having that reference gives me peace on the road that she's actually asleep. I think about it, and it warms my heart to know that I don't have an insecure wife and I don't have to prove myself over and over again. She's given me grace. I have the rope of hope, and I do with it as I please.

Men tell me all the time that their woman accused them of cheating so much, they decided to just do it since she thought they were doing it already. He's like, "If she thinks I'm cheating and she's still here, then I might as well cheat because at least I know she's not going anywhere." That's what I mean by the thing you fear the most coming upon you. My wife doesn't fear me cheating on her, and if she does, she doesn't confess it to me. It's my love for God and my love for her that keep me faithful. Her trust and freedom give me even more strength to live the way I do.

I'm convinced that you have to have trust and freedom in your relationship for it to work long term. If you don't, you'll self-sabotage. Sometimes I want to stir up some fake insecurity, just to laugh at how silly it is to speak from insecurity. I like to tease at times. I'm like, "Oh, I saw you talking to your lil boyfriend over there." She addresses me seriously, and then she realizes I'm just joking, and she laughs me off. For us, it's a moment to remind ourselves that there's no place for insecurity in a healthy relationship. When one of us makes a joke about it, we get to see how silly we looked when we were insecure in our relationship. In today's culture, it's not normal to have so much trust and freedom in a relationship, but that's what healthy love should look like. If you have it, appreciate it and don't do anything to jeopardize it. If you don't have it, please know that it exists and it's possible to have a pure and healthy love.

Sometimes I fear reaping what I've sown. I work so hard trying to right the wrongs of my past so I don't have a nightmare on the way. Then I realize it wouldn't make sense if I reaped what I sowed through my wife. So my past is going to come back to get me in some other way. But that's when I consider grace. You don't have to fear your past if you've accepted God's grace for your life. Yes, you don't deserve the blessings you're about to get, but the grace and love you receive aren't about you; they're about God's promise.

"If we confess our sins, he is faithful and just to forgive us our sins, and to cleanse us from all unrighteousness" 1 John 1:9 (KJV).

As I think of that, I accept the peaceful and stress-free love that I have. It's out there, and I encourage you not to stop until you get it.

My wife can get anything from me because of the way she's positioned her influence in my life. If she said, "Babe, I'd like to take a girl's trip to Europe for a couple of weeks," I'd say, "Okay, babe. Choose your crew and book the trip. I'll hold down the fort until you get back." But guess what? I asked my wife if she'd like to take a writing trip like I'm on right now, and she told me no. I asked her why and she said because she'd be too worried about my parenting skills at home with our sons. Look at that: I'm trying to return the trust and freedom, but her love for home is so strong that being at home feels like a vacation to her. If she wants to take a vacation, she wants it to be with me or as a family. I respect that. I can't say the same, though. Sometimes I need to get away and clear my head. I'm a loner, so I need alone time to talk to God. The men in the Bible went into the wilderness at times to get a download from Heaven. I need to do the same thing to carry out the mission I've been given.

Don't miss out on all the peace and joy in love by getting caught up in fear and insecurity. Let the love flow so you can grow. My wife tells me every time I ask her why she doesn't sweat me about cheating, "If you cheated on me, it would be your loss—not mine." Boom! That floors me! What kind of confidence is that? She doesn't tell me that her world would be over and her heart would be crushed; she tells me it would be my loss. That level of confidence and emotional intelligence has me so wrapped, I don't know what to do. I realize, in her words, that it would be my loss. Of course, she'd be hurt if I betrayed her at this point in our relationship. I know that, but that's not where she puts her mind. She flips it and sees the value in what she brings to the table and how big a loss that would be in my life. She's the reason I'm where I am today, and she understands that. Her influence helped me in my born-again state as a man. Her knowledge of that fact gives her power and peace in being who she's called to be. In that space, you don't have to operate from fear and worry. You can walk in your wholeness and know that you bring the table to the table and God will provide everything else. That's an important place to be in life. That mind-set helped me grow and mature as a man, and I stopped expecting the worst and started preparing for the best. It's a gamble to put all of your hope in trust, but it's worth it. If your man is lying or cheating on you, eventually it will all come to light. You don't have to go digging, searching, and accusing him. Walk in your peace and power, and the rest will be handled. Trust!

Sheri's Perspective

A lot of people have trust issues while in a relationship, but trust issues usually stem from insecurities or past issues. I definitely had my own insecurities from my childhood and early adulthood. As a girl growing up, it's easy to feel like you aren't good enough or worthy if you aren't the most popular. As I got older, I learned that no matter what my past tried to teach me, I was better than that and I was worth more than that. I know I say it over and over again, but learning to truly love yourself is such a necessity. When you get to know yourself and have self-love, you will be less insecure and more confident in yourself. When you have confidence, you will allow yourself to trust people until they give you a reason not to. You understand and value your worth, you realize you are a catch, and you don't feel the need to make sure someone else is realizing your worth. You hope that he does, but realize if he doesn't, he isn't the one for you.

One thing I learned early on is that you can't force someone to love you. And you can't force someone to be faithful to you. Calling someone a million times a day or checking his phone every second won't keep him faithful. If he hasn't given you a reason to be insecure about the relationship, give him the freedom he deserves. I always think about how I want to be treated in a relationship and try to reciprocate that with Tony. I don't want someone accusing me of things I didn't do or calling me twenty times a day to verify my whereabouts. Controlling behavior is not cute and is actually a big turn-off. When you learn to value yourself, you realize you are better than that kind of behavior. You have to be okay with giving your partner freedom and seeing what he does with it. If you give him his freedom and then he does something inappropriate, that should tell you he isn't deserving of your love and trust. When that happens, you have to realize that it's his character flaw, not yours. Just like you can't prevent someone from cheating, you also are never the reason he cheats. If someone decides to cheat in a relationship, that's a choice he made independently of anything you have said or done.

Another huge part of trusting someone is dating someone with the right values to begin with. If you choose someone who doesn't have the right morals and character to begin with, it's pretty hard to expect something different during your relationship. A lot of people put such a high standard on physical things like height or how a person looks that they neglect to really focus on their character traits. Don't get me wrong; being attracted to someone is great, but if his character is ugly, you'll realize the importance of those character traits. Of course, if you can find someone with both, you've found a winner.

The other thing is that once the trust in a relationship is lost, there is no point trying to stay in it. It just doesn't work. Sometimes something happens and we "forgive" the person, but for some reason we just can't forget it. Believe me, I get it, but if you can't forget it and eventually move forward with a clean slate, the relationship can't move forward. Sometimes you have to be okay with forgiving and forgetting the relationship. Trust is the foundation of every relationship, and neither party will be happy without it.

KEY TAKEAWAYS

+ In a relationship, trust is nonnegotiable.
+ You must address your past pain in order to be able to trust someone else.
+ In a relationship, emotional intelligence and self-confidence are contagious.
+ Don't accuse or be overbearing; give your partner trust and freedom until he or she shows you otherwise.
+ Choose someone with the right values to start with.

Chapter 16

SEX IS A PLUS

Most men curse me out when I say this in public. I have to explain myself because it's much deeper than the surface statement. We've placed so much value on sex in our society for no good reason. What is sex? Why does it matter so much? Is it oxygen? There are people who go years without sex, and nothing is lost in their lives. I once thought sex was a priority, but I have enough experience in my past to know that is a lie. I won't go into just how much sin I was in before I rededicated my life to Christ, but for me to have come to this conclusion, you'll have to trust me.

We often call sex "lovemaking," but sexual attraction starts in the mind. The largest sexual organ, therefore, is the mind. Sex is not "lovemaking"; communication is. Sex is the expression of lust. It's the fulfilling of the desire from lust. Lovemaking starts in the mind through conversation and spending quality time together. That is how real love is formed. If you converse enough with a person, you will fall in love with him or her. The love can be romantic love, or it can be platonic love. Once you truly fall in love with someone, you will learn that the greatest feeling isn't sex; it's the other person's presence. Sex can be a downer once you fall in love. The feeling of pleasure is so fleeting that the only thing of substance is the other person's love—not sex. Sex is everything when you have nothing else. When you have true love, sex is something, but it's not everything.

People always say it's so important because if you don't have sexual chemistry, then you have nothing. That's not true. Sexual chemistry comes from having an equal desire for each other—nothing more and nothing less. If you desire each other and then you fall in love with each other, there will be sexual chemistry.

Think about this scenario: You fall in love with someone, and the two of you get married. Everything is amazing, including the sex. Twenty years into your marriage, your spouse has a stroke. The ability and the desire to have sex and enjoy sex are lost. What do you do? Do you leave the love of your life because there is no sex? Do you stop loving your spouse because there is no sex? Do you wither away and die because you can't have sex? Does your spouse die an early death because he or she can't have sex? If your love ends because you can't have sex, you never had real love. I've seen strokes end relationships. I've seen chemotherapy end relationships. Why? Because there was no real love; there was only sex. Sex has only the power you give it. If you understand what love is, sex will lose the power to control you.

Is sex important? Yes, it's important. A man wants that release at times, and so does a woman. The release isn't a necessary function of life, however. It's a craving you have after you've experienced it. The same chemical reaction happens when you have a sexual release as when you take drugs. It's not a necessity; it's an addiction. You're addicted to the feeling. That same feeling can come from anything or anyone you love. Making money feels better than sex for some people. Hitting a home run feels better than sex for some baseball players. Scoring a touchdown feels better than sex for some football players. It's only a chemical release from your brain that tells you it is pleasurable. If your sensory system is damaged, that release will have no effect on your life. It's mental—not physical. I've been highly sexually active in my past, and my life was not better than it is now. If sex was the key, then everyone who is highly active sexually would be rich, famous, extremely happy, and successful. Sex has only the power you give it.

I urge you to find a deeper purpose in love. Find a deeper purpose in a relationship. Life happens, and sex can't always be in it. I learned this after I got married. Things change when a woman goes through seasons in her life. After having a child, she's instructed to wait six weeks before engaging in intercourse. If you're accustomed to having sex eighteen times over a period of six weeks, that's a drastic difference. If you're accustomed to doing anything eighteen times over a six-week period, to reduce it to zero is a major adjustment. In that period of time, if you're faithful and loving on your new child, you'll learn that sex isn't everything. Sex is a plus—not a priority. That's your first lesson.

Then you go through another experience of feeding the baby. The baby has to eat every two hours. Then it's every four hours. This goes on for months. If a woman is breastfeeding, she's either pumping or feeding the baby from her breast every few hours. I challenge every man to set an alarm clock to wake up every two hours, get up, exert yourself physically, and then lie back down, only to get up again in ninety minutes. What woman do you think will want to have sex after twenty-four hours of that life? When our first son came home after spending three months in the neonatal intensive care unit, he was on a feeding tube. He had to be fed every couple of hours. The bag that held his food had to be prepared, then washed out after use. A feeding took probably thirty minutes, and then we had to wake up in ninety minutes to do it all over again. I literally almost lost my mind. My wife and I almost lost our minds together. It was one of the most stressful things I've ever had to do in my life, and I didn't give birth to him. That was another season when I learned that sex is not a priority. Love is the priority.

Then other things happen in life, and it alters your lovemaking schedule. My wife lives with migraines or headaches in certain seasons. It's genetic for her. If you've ever had a migraine, sex is the last thing you want. In these seasons, I have learned that sex is not a priority.

Then there is surgery. My wife had lower back surgery once and was on bed rest for eight weeks. That was longer than the no-sex period after giving birth. Seeing her in pain, loving her, and watching her suffer through the recovery, I learned that sex is not a priority. You don't know what you can do until love requires it of you. We have to stop putting so much power in things that don't really matter in the grand scheme.

I'll be honest with you: I'm at a place in my life where I'd rather spend quality time with my wife than have sex with her. Yes, sex is amazing when you go there, but it's not everything when you tap into real love. The conversation, the hugs, the laughs, the gentle caress, the deep eye contact—that's what love is all about. Look at the big picture of love. It's a marathon, and there comes a time when it will lose its importance in your life naturally. If you've made it everything up until that point, you will have nothing when your body takes a turn in maturity. What is sex at seventy? What is sex at eighty? If you don't know the meaning of true love by then, what will you have when you reach that point?

I'd like for society to shift the focus from sex to love. Men and women say all the time that you have to try it before marriage because what if you get married and it's not good? It's impossible for the simple act of sex not to be pleasurable if you're in love. It's physically, mentally, and spiritually impossible to be a bad experience if you are truly in love. I've discovered this for myself. Until you have true love—a sacrificial and selfless love—you cannot say that this isn't true.

When you're not in love, sex can last thirty minutes to an hour. When you fall in love, the way the mind processes the presence of the person you love, sex is done before it even starts. Your mind is so powerful and it's already wrapped up in the person you love that the simple touch and connection with their body sends your body into ecstasy. Not much has to be done. There are no tricks of the trade that need to be performed when you're truly in love. It's mental. I'm talking thirty to ninety seconds, and the release is mutual, with nothing else left to be desired. That is the benefit of real love. By real love, I mean two people who are 100 percent committed and faithful to each other. The two beings are sold on the idea of love and basking in the reality of its power.

It can't be one person in and the other person out. It won't work if she's deeply in love with him but he isn't deeply in love with her. If it's not a selfless and sacrificial love, the connection I speak of will not be there. The reason so many people place so much emphasis on sex is that they've never made the sacrifice to love on the level I'm writing about in this chapter. If you've had only microwave love, this may not make complete sense. I'm speaking of a love where both parties are fully engaged and devoted to each other. That is where the divine happens. It's at that point you realize why sex was created. It's an expression of lust, but it's not the essence of love. This I know for a fact because I've been on both sides of the phenomenon. I would not lie about something so spiritual and powerful. I do not have the full vocabulary to express the feeling of loving on this level. It takes true personal sacrifice to reach this level. The efforts must be mutual, and the relationship must be sexually secure without any outside influences or distractions. If the man or the woman gives in to outside lust or engages in any form of emotional or physical cheating, the chemistry will be lost. This level of love is more natural for a woman than it is for a man because she was created for love. As men learn to love and be 100 percent faithful, this next level of the sexual experience is tapped into. It's not something that money can buy. The man who has had the most women can't tell you about this experience. Only the men who have suppressed their youthful lust for multiple women and given their heart to one woman can understand the experience I'm describing. I would not trade this level of love and understanding for the world.

There are times of frustration when your love is devouring your voice and you can't express it to the level you wish, but that frustration is a reminder of the power of love. Although it can be confusing at times, it's followed by a peace that reminds you that love conquers all. The expression of your love is a marathon, not a sprint. You'd like to consume your woman with your love, but it's not possible because the love is infinite and boundless. It unlocks your life in levels you did not know were possible. Clarity and peace that follow this type of love, and everything in you is transformed. The words you speak will be like parables or mysteries to those who hear you because so few men have allowed their hearts to be given to a love this pure. It's hard to grasp until you surrender to it. There are no shortcuts.

Real love is oven baked—not microwaved. It will take time, commitment, and sacrifice. If you want to do it any other way, you'll miss the mark. This should not be a mystery, and I urge every man who reads this to commit fully to the process. I urge the women who have been given to youthful lust and the confusion of sex to reconsider the meaning of it all. Allow your heart to fall in love in purity and not in lust. Love is greater than lust. Although they can coincide, lust will never outweigh the power of love. True love is everlasting and has to be approached and appreciated as such. If you try to rush it, you will ruin it. If you measure love based on the fulfillment of lust, you'll miss the mark every time. Love can't be measured or predicted by the level of chemistry you have with someone based on lust alone. True sexual chemistry comes from a selfless and sacrificial love, nothing more. If you take your time and you respect the process, it will work in your favor. If at any time you try to rush the process or skip the steps, you will be left in dissatisfaction. I've been there, and my frustration led me to force the feeling and push for the lust, and it never worked as I planned. But when I relax in the arms of true love and take my time making love to the mind, the body soon follows. It's mental and spiritual. It is not physical. It doesn't matter your strength, size, or experience is. If you don't have real love, you will be lacking. Sacrifice and selflessness are the key. Be all in. Be fully committed to love, and it will be everything you dreamed of it being and much more. It takes two to make it happen. Love is so much more than sex. A relationship is so much more than sex. Trust the process of love, and watch your dreams come true. No one will be able to fully explain it to you. The experience of real love will create its own meaning and purpose in your life. Even your explanation of it will fall short, but I can tell you that it's real and anyone can have it. Love is the greatest gift given to mankind—not sex. Love is not sex, and sex is not love. When you understand that, everything in your relationship will change for the better.

Sheri's Perspective

Anytime Tony talks about this, he gets so much backlash. People assume he is saying that we don't have sex or that sex means nothing. We have two kids, so obviously the former isn't true, and we all know the latter isn't true because we're talking about it in this book. Thinking about it, I realize that most people aren't really in love and so that's why they don't get it.

So let's be clear: a relationship is so much more than sex, and if it isn't in your relationship, that's where the problem lies. Sexual attraction or lust can be a fleeting thing. Lust and sexual attraction are usually based on physical appearance initially. People change, bodies change, schedules change, so if the glue that holds the relationship together is having sex, the relationship will fall apart. Have you noticed that a lot of couples are blissfully happy in the dating phase and even the first couple years of marriage. They have their first baby, maybe the wife puts on a little bit of weight, she is unimaginably exhausted, and now their marriage is on the brink and headed toward divorce. What happened to that once over-the-moon happy couple? They fell in lust, not love. Lust changes with the seasons and doesn't stand the test of time. If a woman gains five pounds, lust is looking for the next person who is more in shape. If you are exhausted from breastfeeding or staying up with the baby, lust looks for the woman who has more time. Lust can jump from person to person in a blink of an eye. Lust can't stand the test of time.

When you truly fall in love with someone, it's a lot different. Love is staying up all night talking twelve years into marriage as if you are high school sweethearts. Love is going without sex for long periods of time because of pregnancies or medical issues and not missing a beat. Love is truly being each other's best friend through every up and down. Love is actively listening to each other in every conversation. Love is having mutual respect for each other and never intentionally tearing each other down. Love isn't perfect, but with both people actively putting in an effort, it can feel pretty close. When you are truly and happily in love, you begin to understand how ice cream is the foundation of your relationship. It's the core reason you fell in love with each other years ago. It's the reason you have stayed in love through different seasons of life. It's the reason you would stay by the other person's side through anything even if it required your sacrifice.

When your foundation is that strong, sex can only be the cherry on top. The cherry is a great addition and makes the ice cream even better, but if it happens to fall off for whatever reason, the ice cream will still be good.

If it makes no sense to you that sex is a plus, not a priority, I hope you will understand one day. It doesn't mean sex isn't great and a great addition to a relationship, but when you find out how to truly love someone, you will understand that it can't be the foundation of your relationship. We aren't telling people never to have sex; rather, we're encouraging people to fall in love with someone without sex and you will see how much better your relationship will be. You will also see how much better your sex life is when you are truly in love and not just in lust.

KEY TAKEAWAYS

+ Don't place so much value on sex; it's not what a real relationship is built on.
+ If you understand what love is, sex will lose the power to control you.
+ Sex is a plus, not a priority (it's the cherry on top of the ice cream of your relationship).
+ Real love is oven baked—not microwaved.

Chapter 17

YOU'RE NOT A MAID

I was trapped by society's depiction of a woman in the home. Deep down, I wanted that from my woman because it seemed like the easy life. Imagine being poor but still being able to afford a chef, maid, butler, nanny, and every other service worker possible. That's essentially what so many women are to men today. I've spoken with women who have four children and cook a hot meal every day. Some women have told me in coaching sessions that they've never turned their man down when he wanted sex, no matter what time of day or night it was. To hear the lives of some women floored me. I'd hear stories of the royal treatment some women give men, only to be cheated on in return. In so many coaching sessions, I sat there jealous. Yes, the grown boy tried to surface sometimes and I wanted the life other men have. Then it hit me: That's not right. A woman isn't a maid.

Yes, there were times in the past when money was not as easily made as it is today. Fast food couldn't be found on every corner. Life was much slower, and the world wasn't as advanced. The days of women doing every single chore around the house should be long gone because the world has changed so much. It costs much more to live, and many women are working forty hours a week outside the home, just like their men. If a woman's job is staying home with the children, it actually can be less fun and more demanding than a job outside the home. I've stayed at home with my sons all day, and it's a lot of work. I remember chasing after my sons and having to keep an eye on them every second of the day. It was very draining. As much as I love my sons, it's hard watching a little human nonstop. If you turn your head, the dog is covered in Vaseline—true story. Close your eyes too long, you look up and all the keys have been plucked off the laptop keyboard and your son has spelled his name with the keys—true story. Kids are demanding, and they rule the world. Your world doesn't belong to you anymore. You become the child's maid, and you don't have a choice. Once a woman has children to take care of, everything about her role in a man's mind should change. The children become the priority. Life starts to run together, and things just aren't as seamless as you thought they'd be.

There was a part of me that hoped my wife could be a superhuman and do everything while keeping the earth in balance on its spinning axis. It's just not realistic to think that way. It's also not fair. Growing up, I'd always hear my mom yell at my dad, "I work forty hours just like you do." It's funny to me today, but at the time, I didn't understand her point. I was trapped in the typical male mind-set that a woman should do everything. My mom wasn't having it. Today, my wife has a schedule, and our sons come first. Kids come first because they can't fend for themselves. I know you're thinking that I should come first, but it's not realistic. Fact is, I'm a grown man. I can do everything I need done for myself. If my wife only has time to do for me or do for our sons, I'd want her to choose them every time.

In a typical week, sometimes after doing everything for my kids, there may not be much left in her tank. After our boys are in bed, we may kick around and shoot the breeze until midnight or later. My wife wakes up at 5:30 every morning to pack lunches, iron clothes, and get things situated for the boys. That means she's running off of five hours of sleep most of the time. After a week of that, it starts to catch up with you and things get foggy. Our son's school is about a forty-minute drive from our home. That means every morning, five days a week, my wife fights traffic for eighty minutes in the morning and eighty minutes in the afternoon. Driving is very taxing on the body because it requires a lot of focus and mental energy. If you're running behind, that induces anxiety and stress when you're a perfectionist like my wife. If you add up 160 minutes on the road, five days a week, you'll see that a good amount of her life is spent driving.

Everything affects everything else, so if she didn't have a full night's rest, that's going to carry over when she gets back home from dropping them off. There are other things that have to be done while they're in school, whether you work from home or report to a job. The fatigue is setting in and running over. After my wife gets home from dropping our sons off, she has about five hours to work out, handle emails, do post office drops, take a nap, get her personal stuff done, and get things ready for band, swim, soccer, yoga, or whatever other after-school activities the boys have. The time flies by, and before you know it, she's back on the road to pick them up from school. After driving for eighty minutes in afternoon traffic, the last thing you want to do is come home and start cooking. Even if you wanted to, you can't because homework has to be done and Dad might not be the go-to guy for homework.

The one and only time I helped my son on his math homework because my wife was out of town, he got a D on the assignment. I retired from homework after that. I take our older son to soccer practice, and my wife takes the younger to his sport. No one is home to watch the stove, and food can't cook itself. It's fast food or cook when you get back home after practice. After driving another hour to and from practice, you're exhausted because you've made three round-trips for your children that day, and you have to find the energy to do it all again tomorrow. Let's say you found time to cook. Wow, you're superwoman. But who's going to wash the dishes? If your man was raised like I was, as a spoiled athlete, his domestic skills may not be where they need to be and you'd rather brave it alone. I've tried to wash dishes, and my wife always comes and stops me midway and tells me she'd rather do it because I miss too many spots. I don't believe that's true, but I'm not going to argue with her about something I'm not that excited about doing anyway. If she's supertired, she'll let me do the dishes.

I'm battling in my mind with all of society's messages to me about a woman being everything to the man and the kids, and it's hard for me to get into doing dishes and cleaning up the kitchen. My wife doesn't have an outside job, so I also tell myself that I'm the breadwinner because I'm listening to all the things I've heard men say for decades. All of the brainwashing that ruins relationships is playing over and over in the minds of both men and women. A lot of women feel they are supposed to be able to do it all and not feel tired. Then they beat themselves up for being human and getting tired while trying to be everything to everyone and nothing to themselves. This is the life in our world today. So many women have become shells of themselves trying to uphold an unrealistic standard of womanhood. It's also embarrassing to women if they fall short of that standard. Instead of owning with pride that they're human just like men, they get down on themselves and would rather it be a secret. We've introduced every extracurricular activity the mind can conceive for children to do, and then we expect every night to end with a well-balanced, nutritious meal after you've taken four children to four different practices or one child to a gymnastics practice that lasted four hours.

We've created unrealistic standards. In the 1950s, when women cooked, did laundry, cleaned tile grouting with toothbrushes, and ironed everyone's clothes for a week at a time, it wasn't like it is today. Could women even vote? Were there any female CEOs? Women barely had an identity or a voice, if we're being honest. Principles remain the same even when times change, but a woman being a housemaid to her husband and children isn't a principle; it's a societal condition put into place by man. Some things have to change, and I believe that the expectation of women to be superhuman is one of them.

I had to slap myself in the face with no baby powder. I needed to feel the cold reality of life today. There was an understanding I had to come to, and that is the fact that my wife is human just like I am. Do I feel like doing all that she does? No, I do not feel like doing half of what she does. Therefore, should I expect her to execute everything flawlessly and with complete consistency? No, I cannot expect that after knowing the human limitations and all the pressure put on us today. Seventy years ago is a very long time. It's twice as long as I've been alive. The children back then did not have to be driven forty minutes to school and then to soccer, baseball, piano, gymnastics, softball, volleyball, football, band, robotics club, chess club, golf, tennis, synchronized swimming, choir club, and everything else. Those are actual things my sons and their friends are into these days. My niece has gymnastics practice every day for four hours. On top of that practice, she still has to do homework and have a normal life. Our technology and advancements have put us into a bind, and we have to change with the times. Adjustments and sacrifices have to be made. Some necessary things need to be automated. I ask myself, "Do you prefer to have your wife's peace and sanity or a few extra dollars in the bank?" I'd prefer her peace and sanity any day. So what does that mean? That means I sacrifice and budget so we can afford house cleaners to come once every two weeks. They clean homes for a living, so the precision and perfection they clean our home with is second to none. They've done it for so long, my wife can't come close to doing the job they do because she doesn't have the passion or profession for it like they do. I pay to have groceries delivered each week. That saves my wife eight hours a month. I have a wholesale store membership. That allows my wife to go to the store and get bulk items that last much longer than normal grocery store items. We have a membership in a gym that has a sauna and steam room. The workouts, training sessions, and me time help my wife function better throughout the week. They help her feel loved and appreciated, and they hit the refresh button, which keeps her rejuvenated for the journey ahead. I don't do all those things for the women who clean our home. They clean up as their profession, and they make great money. They take care of their own mental and emotional health. I can't treat my wife like them. My relationship with the house cleaners is based on a business transaction. Your woman is not your cleaning service. She is an investment with a very high return. The return is so high, it's priceless.

By not settling for the unfair standards put on women today, my wife makes me respect her more. It helps me realize that she's a human, not a robot. As men, we forget that. She can earn money just like I can. Women have proven their ability to be high learners and high earners. How many men are able to manage a household with the efficiency of a woman? I believe if we have a mutual respect for each other and we get rid of the gender roles, we can flourish as couples.

Some expectations need to be thrown out. Others need to be divided up, depending on your situation. It may make sense in your home for everything to remain the same as society has instituted. If that's what works and everyone is happy with it, don't change it. On the other hand, if you see there's a need for some change to make the household better, don't be afraid of that change. There's a term "soccer mom," but guess what? I'm a "soccer dad." I actually see more dads at practice than moms now. Yes, some moms are home getting dinner ready, but others are still working or at another practice with another child. I could say, "I have to work, so I need to stay home." Instead, I take my son to practice, and I coach my six o'clock client from the comfort of my car. I sit and idle my car with the air-conditioning on for an hour with my laptop on the center console, typing notes as my client is talking to me. It's a sacrifice, but I make it work. I could be difficult and tell my wife that I must coach my client in the comfort of my office and have her add another round trip to her to-do list, but that's not right. It's time we rewrite some of the rules and spread the word. If women could become less maids who aren't fully appreciated and more wives and mothers who have normal lives, our world would be a better place. A woman can take on as many tasks as she pleases, but let it be because it makes sense to her and it's what she feels is her fair share. Don't make it a forced situation that drains her of emotion and reduces her to a robotic lifestyle devoid of joy and fulfillment. I'm seeing far too many mummies instead of mommies walking around.

You're not a maid.

Sheri's Perspective

I was not raised in a household where I was taught how to be a wife. For a lot of my life, my mom was a single mom. When I was young, we came to the United States from Jamaica, and my mom worked really hard to try to create a better life for me. She worked two jobs to provide for me. I played a lot of sports throughout school and was expected to maintain good grades. I fell in love with medicine at a young age, so that was my goal. I would get home really late from practices and games in high school, so my mom would've picked up something to eat. When my mom was married to my stepdad, my stepdad would cook most nights and my mom would cook only on the weekends. Between sports and school, I wasn't expected to cook, and it was never a rule for me. Of course, as I got older and in college, I would call my mom and grandma to give me a recipe if I wanted to cook something, but it was never a priority for me growing up. I never grew up in a household that followed society's old-school standards, so those were never ingrained in me.

When I got married and had kids, of course some things did change. At first, I tried to do things like society expected because I thought that it was what a wife was supposed to do. I was like a zombie trying to keep everything in pristine condition, and I realized I had to give myself grace. Grace is the word for me during this season of life. I have talked about it and posted about it a few times on social media. We have to get over trying to look perfect and stop comparing ourselves to other people who seem to have life all together. If I look on Instagram, maybe there is a mom who looks to have a superclean house and cooks dinner every single night. We have to realize that everyone's life is different and social media always portray someone's highlights reel.

Our kids are very active and keep us extremely busy. Our oldest plays every sport imaginable for his school but also plays on an elite travel soccer team and plays ten months out of the year. We were literally in a hotel for soccer almost every weekend this year. Most days I pick up my younger son first after his yoga or Lego club finishes and then wait for my older to finish practice and then rush him home to grab a snack and change clothes so he can head to his travel soccer practice. Then my younger needs to go to swim, baseball, or soccer practice. Sometimes I will have had time to cook something in the Crock-Pot or put together a quick meal after we get back, but there a lot of times we are both exhausted and will order food on the way home. Whatever works for your family, don't be embarrassed or ashamed by it. Give yourself grace. Don't spend so much time trying to create the perfect image you think society demands that you miss out on living and enjoying life. There are some nights when I have loads of laundry to fold but Tony just got in from out of town so I'll choose to spend time with him over laundry. If it works for your family for you to cook and clean every day, that's great and something to be proud of, too. Every family is set up is differently; I choose not to have a nanny or regular babysitter, so my energy is focused there. I would rather hire someone for my deep cleanings twice a month than miss a soccer weekend to stay home and get that done. But whatever your setup is, give yourself grace and give others grace, too. Be less judgmental and more supportive, because we are all doing our best, and that's what is important.

KEY TAKEAWAYS

✦ Both people can help with the housework and the kids.

✦ Get help whenever and wherever you need it.

✦ Women should not be expected to be superhuman.

✦ Give yourself grace; live by the standards that work for you, not those society has led you to believe are right.

Chapter 18

SILENCE IS GOLDEN

There is power in silence. This is an alternative to the 72-Hour Rule. Not everything is worth going silent for three full days, but there is still a lot of power in intermittent silence. This is not a mind game, either. This is silence coming from a place of peace and self-love. Your desire is to bring peace—not cause more problems.

There are many techniques that relate to this type of silence. Think all the way back to being a kid and being put into time-out. The isolation and silence were intended to induce thoughts about why you did what you did and why you shouldn't do it anymore. You get a chance to miss your friends and your interactions. The lingering feeling of disappointment from your parent or teacher also stings you in the heart. The feeling isn't one you want to feel often. You want to be included in playtime and be able to enjoy life just like everyone else. A time-out helps achieve that goal. Yes, there are some special cases of people who seem to love a time-out, but most people hate it. My five-year-old son has been in time-out maybe once all school year, and we have only a month left. The reason he stays out of trouble is that he doesn't want to miss any fun with his friends. I can count on two hands how many times he's had to be in time-out at home. The love is consistent, and the correction is consistent. It teaches lessons from the start and sets the tone for future behavior. The same thing goes for relationships. You have to set the tone early. Any behavior you reinforce will repeat itself. Any behavior you stop will decrease.

You can also find lessons similar to these in behavioral science. My wife and I worked in a group home with adult men who had mental disabilities. I worked there for five years. My wife was there maybe a year or two. While working there, we learned a technique called "ignore—redirect—reinforce." We also learned one called "stop—redirect—reinforce." My wife learning those techniques was one of the worst and best things to happen in our relationship. The "ignore" technique is to be used when the client isn't exhibiting dangerous behavior, yet still has attention-seeking behavior. The "stop" technique is to be used when the client is exhibiting behavior that can harm you or him. My wife used the "stop" technique once when I tried to yell at her while we were dating, which I mentioned earlier in the book. Ironically, I think that was before she started working at the group home. Since then, she's used the "ignore" technique on me to perfection. It really works. This is where silence works.

If a man has an attitude for reasons that have nothing to do with you, you have to ignore him. If he speaks to you in a way you don't like, after calmly checking him, you have to ignore him. To ignore, in this context, doesn't mean you ignore him completely. What it means is to reduce communication to what is absolutely necessary. "Are you hungry?" "Would you like some of the dinner I've made?" "Will you be able to pick up the kids from school?" "Are you able to take your son to practice?" Those are necessary questions. "How are you doing today?" "What time does the game come on?" "Did you see the new headline today?" Those are not necessary questions. Outside of the necessary questions, it's absolute silence. The silence appears peaceful for you because you're going through your normal routine. Anything your man doesn't respond to or won't do, you keep it moving as if he had given you an answer. Any slack he leaves, you pick it up without complaint and send a silent message to him that he's not as needed as he thinks he is. The peace and silence are very disturbing and loud for the man on the receiving end. In his mind, the silence shifts the atmosphere and everything feels different. The man starts to get fidgety and worried. *Is she getting over me? Is she tired of me? Have I added the straw that broke her back? What's next?* The silence becomes deafening in his ears. The fact that it looks so peaceful for you makes it even worse. If you were slamming things down, sucking your teeth, and making noise to get attention, it would be satisfying to the man to know he's under your skin. But when you're silent and peaceful, it drives him crazy because he's left to his own thoughts without reassurance that everything is going to be all right. This is where his brain starts to coach him, trying to help him self-soothe. Now everything you wanted to say to him, he's saying to himself. He knows what you'd say anyway, so he starts preaching to himself and teaching himself how to act. But because it's coming from the wrong place for him, it doesn't last. He goes back to being antsy and wanting things to go back to normal. He knows that what he did or said was wrong and he has to make it right. If he wants the energy of the house to return to normal, he has to cut through the silence with an apology. This requires him to admit to his guilt and apologize for what he said or did to you. When you accept his apology graciously, he moves at a different frequency because he wants it to be a long time before the deafening silence returns.

During the silence, he watches how you move about the house with peace and poise. He's confused as to how you can function with silence. He starts talking to himself. *Is she that strong? Does she think she did nothing wrong? Is she not going to accept the fault and guilt and apologize to me for what I did wrong? Does she not care enough to break the silence herself just to get things back to normal? What if I give her a taste of her own medicine and stay silent for a week? Can she handle it?* All of those questions run through his mind. Then he realizes: *I was wrong for how I spoke to her. I could have made my point in a better way. The goal of what I was trying to accomplish was lost because of the way I spoke down to her. I wanted her to know how I was feeling and what was on my mind, but I expressed it from the wrong place. I have to do better next time. She's a good woman, and I know she loves me. Everything in her wants to be the best woman she can be, and I need to appreciate that about her. She doesn't give me any real problems. Most of the stuff I say she does, I'm making up in my head. I have to do better. She deserves better, and if I don't get it together, one day she's going to find someone better. Man, I hope this isn't the time she decides she's fed up with my mess. What if she leaves me in a week or two? What will I do to get her back? This is too much. I have to end this silence and get her back to normal. These voices in my head are driving me crazy, and she looks like she doesn't have a care in the world. Does she have another man waiting on her? I'm tripping. I know she loves me and she's faithful. Let me end this right now and break the silence with a sincere apology and see what it does.*

All of that goes through his mind, and that's what pushes him to open up and make things right. Yes, some men have egos so big, they can really give you a run for your money. I've heard women tell me it's been silent two to four weeks in their home. There are men who won't bend or break. That's a sign that standards weren't set from the start. If things get too bad, you may have to realize that and come up with an alternate plan.

Silence is healing. When you're silent, you allow the work to do itself. God steps in and starts to speak. The mind is cluttered, but clarity cuts through in the silence. The thoughts can be heard, but even more, they can be *felt*. Silence is golden because it pierces the heart in a way that words can't. The best or the worst talk is always self-talk. In moments of silence, there will be both, but the good will win. You have to be willing to let silence speak, especially when your words don't seem to be enough. It takes strength to be silent, but it rewards you in the end. If it's meant to be, it will be. You can't fear silence, or it will destroy you. Let it work *for* you instead of working *against* you. There is peace in silence. So much energy is drawn from that space. What is meditation? There's peace in silence, and once you learn how to channel that instead of arguing all the time, you get a lot more done with much better results. Silence does the heavy lifting and cuts through the noise with a clear message that whips hearts into shape. I've been both the victim and the beneficiary of silence over and over again. By being silent, you create a break in the chaos without taking an actual break. If you take too many breaks, you'll lose your relationship. But you can use silence to your benefit without having to leave the relationship. Your presence with silence is a powerful combination, and it yields great results if you love the right person. So next time you need to be heard, try being silent. You don't have to yell, curse, fuss, and fight. You can embrace silence and let it speak on your behalf. It doesn't hurt to look sexy in your silence, either. It gives the man a chance to see and hear what he's missing. He wants that energy back. He's craving the connection with your spirit again. Your silence is deafening, and he's beginning to hear clearly because of it. The decibels are peaking, and he's ready for his peace back. You are his peace, but you can't be his peace if you can't be silent at times. Don't get used up and taken advantage of by the nature of a man who is accustomed to conquering everyone in his way. Instead, stand your ground and match his energy with the power of silence.

Let peace ring loud in your home by harnessing the power within you. For so long, we've thought that it's our voice that has all the power, but in certain situations, your silence speaks so much louder. Each time you use the power, you'll understand it better. You'll begin to realize that it shouldn't be used or abused but lived through. It's for you as much as it is for him. You'll grow and become better in your silence. The self-evaluation in the process will help you meet your man halfway, and when you start speaking again, both of you will be better for the short season of silence you've experienced. This lesson will go down in the history books of love as one of the greatest lessons ever taught to mankind, and I learned it from a woman's influence in my life.

Sheri's Perspective

Sometimes being silent is the best way to handle things, in my opinion. When you are angry, if you respond right away, you can say things you didn't mean and cause more issues than what you started with. Very early on in our relationship, when Tony would get snappy or respond in a way I didn't appreciate, I would give him my version of the silent treatment. It was definitely based on the behavior psychology techniques we learned while working in a group home. While in the group home, I was promoted to behavior specialist, so I was writing behavior plans for developmentally disabled men, and I got to see the data on how the techniques worked in different situations. Some of the techniques stuck, and the "ignore—redirect" technique was and is still one of my favorites.

This is for situations that are just attention seeking and don't require a real conversation. It's usually when one of us is getting an attitude for no reason or really snappy in a way that the other doesn't appreciate. So, for example, if Tony is in a bad mood and kind of snappy about things that don't really matter, I see that as attention-seeking behavior and I don't reinforce it. Anything you reinforce will continue. It doesn't necessarily require me addressing it with him, because most times he already knows he is being snappy. I ignore the behavior, but I don't engage with him about it because that attention just reinforces the behavior. People don't realize that even negative attention is attention. I continue with the day as if nothing has happened. I am not engaging in frivolous conversation with him, but I am still talking to him, and I continue to be happy and content as if nothing is bothering me. I will ask him if he is ready for dinner or questions like that but nothing extra. The goal is for him to feel that I don't appreciate the behavior and also realize that it's not going to get the result he expected. His attitude isn't going to affect my attitude. Once a person realizes that you aren't going to be affected by their behavior, you will start to see less and less of that behavior from them.

It works the same way for the kids. I remember when my older son was very little, he had a tantrum and decided to fall out crying when we were at the house. He fell onto the ground and was crying, trying to get his way. I acted as if nothing had happened, stepped over him, and continued doing what I was doing around the house. After a few minutes of crying and realizing I wasn't there, he stopped crying and came up to me. In that moment, I explained to him that that's not how you get what you want from Mommy. That was the first and last time he ever threw a tantrum.

A lot of the time, we don't realize we are reinforcing negative behaviors in our relationship by snapping back or giving the behavior the attention the other person is looking for. Sometimes we can accomplish more with silence than we can with words. It takes a lot of maturity to handle things this way, but I promise you, it's very effective. It's much easier to snap back and get into an argument, but if you can learn to recognize the behavior as attention seeking and nothing personal against you, it's easier to have no visible response to it. Of course, different situations that require different approaches; this is just for the small and petty things that can build up and cause bigger arguments when not handled properly. So next time you feel like something is a little off, try ignoring the behavior, and that will help redirect the behavior both in the moment and in the future.

HOW AND WHEN TO USE SILENCE

+ Silence is a great way to address attention-seeking behavior.
+ Examples of attention-seeking behavior include a bad attitude and snappy responses.
+ Don't respond with the same behavior.
+ Recognize the other person's behavior and ignore it.
+ Continue in the same positive way as if nothing the other person has said or done has bothered you.
+ When negative behavior isn't reinforced (given attention), its frequency tends to decrease.

Chapter 19

DON'T COMPETE

One of the worst things I've seen happening over the last few years is the number of women competing with men. In a lot of cities, women outnumber the men by a large margin. That causes some desperation in many women. When the race for a husband starts, all standards go out the window. It becomes a game for the man who has multiple women knowingly competing for his love. At first it was an accident. A man doesn't typically tell a woman that there are many others competing for him. It's something that most men keep a secret while trying to make each woman feel that she's the only one. The times he can't be available, he pretends it's because of his busy work schedule and not because of another woman. Eventually, it comes out that there's another woman. I'm not sure what actually happens at this point that makes some women decide to compete and win, but it's happening at alarming rates.

When you compete for a man's love, he loses all respect for you. He actually starts to lose respect for himself as well. His journey to becoming a good man comes to a screeching halt, and he becomes a dog instead. Now he's the playah from the Himalayas—in his mind—and all logic and reason leave him. It's now time to see just how deep he can get the game to go. Every ounce of insecurity he has is being fed right now. All of the times he was rejected and overlooked by the women he wanted, it's all payback now. He's going to be the biggest player to ever do it. It's game time. He puts a system into place to give each woman just enough to feel like she has him and she's winning the competition. The pursuit for a wife is put on hold because this game is too much fun. He's not considering anyone's heart, not even his own. All he's thinking about is lust and how to fulfill it. It gets really nasty. If you're sexually active with a man when you know he's dealing with another woman, you're making a bed of nails that you'll have to lie on at some point. Now you're having unprotected sex with him. He's literally coming from one woman unprotected straight to you unprotected. There's a concoction of bacteria brewing in the worst places. The Good Book does say, "The wages of sin is death." In this case, the love triangle is working on manifesting a deadly sexually transmitted disease. Yes, it happens every day. I don't think most women think about the fact that men are sleeping with multiple women unprotected, and in most cases, it happens the same day. I cannot count how many times a woman has written me and said she's pregnant by a guy, but he also has another woman pregnant. In many cases, I hear about the incurable herpes disease that was contracted in the process. It's getting very real out here in the dating field, and consequences are piling up pretty high. The man participating in the dating chaos isn't thinking clearly. It's such a rush to him. He's feeding his ego and not considering the children he'll have to split time with and provide for the rest of his life.

Men have so many insecurities that most of them will allow multiple women to compete for their love. There's still this king mentality some men have that makes them feel as if a woman should compete for their love. You have to know who you are as a woman and not be willing to compete.

I've noticed that a woman who competes for a man's love shrinks and starts to forget her worth. Her value isn't gone; she just forgets what she's worth. Desperation sets in, and she tells herself that this is the way it has to be done if she's going to get her man. I've coached women in this situation, and it's sad to hear their thought process. If you're the woman in that situation, you begin to lose yourself, and now you just want to beat the other woman. It becomes a competition. You're trying to lose weight. The shopping increases. Now you have a gym membership with a personal training package. Your hair and nails are always done. Everything has to be perfect from head to toe. Next come the intimacy and trying to make sure you're putting out more than the other woman is. If that doesn't make you feel secure enough, you start stalking and hunting. You find out where the other woman works, where she lives, and you become obsessed with her. The next thing you know, you're stalking her social media until you get blocked. Now you make a fake account so you can keep lurking. She's posting pictures and subliminal messages for you, and you're doing the same. You'd think the man you're competing for is King Solomon, but no, it's a regular Joe who has a decent job until the company downsizes. He's mediocre at everything he does, from communication to planning a date and everything else. It's not even about him anymore. Now it's about the competition with the other woman to win him. If you happen to win him for a season, you're bored and waiting for the next woman to compete with. It becomes a subconscious expectation, and you start telling yourself you'd have to go through this with any man you date, so you might as well lace up the gloves for this one. It has been worse. There's slicing of the tires. Also, there's the removing of license plates, the busting of windows, and the list goes on. Depending on where you're from and how you were raised, the competition can really get ugly. What lets me know how real it gets is the fact that so many movies and television shows are based on this very thing. Who are you? You don't even know anymore. You're competing for a grown boy, basically. Any man who would make you compete for his love isn't a real man yet. He's just as lost as you are. Two lost people end up in the middle of nowhere with nothing to their names and nowhere else to go. Is it worth it? You're losing yourself for what? For whom? I like all the work you're doing on yourself to look beautiful, but what about your spirit?

A woman of influence will never compete for a man. You can be a woman of influence if you choose to. It's not a once/always situation. You can grow. You can change. If you've found yourself stooping beneath your values and competing for a man's love and attention, you can get back up. Stand up tall, and be the woman you know you were called to be. A man who knows what he wants won't allow women to compete for him. His choice will be made right away if he happens to be talking to multiple women as friends with the potential to become mates. As soon as I met my wife, I cut off every other woman on my phone. I was going back and forth with a toxic woman for two years. It ended immediately after I met my wife. I could tell she wasn't the type to compete for me because she wouldn't even let me compete for her. When I met her, she was in a situation. She didn't entertain me until I spoke to her again after that situation was over. I knew by the way she handled her business that she wasn't going to tolerate being juggled with other women.

You lose all your influence in a man's life when you know he has another woman and you stay with him. He stops respecting you, although he's telling you he still loves you. The lies will increase, and you'll believe him when he tells you that she doesn't mean anything to him and you're his everything. He's telling you that she's crazy and stalking him and he's just trying to let her down easy so she doesn't do anything crazy to him or to you. You're wrapped up in the lies and the games, and it's only going to get worse. You can't influence him at that point, because you can't even influence yourself. Anything you say to him that's positive or worth anything, he doesn't hear. It goes into one ear and out the other. He won't listen to you, because *you* don't listen to you. Everyone knows that you know better than what you're showing, but because you won't listen to the reason and logic, he can't respect your voice, either. Everything is lost, and you're holding on to nothing with a clenched fist. The relationship isn't worth anything, even if you stick around forever. If a man allows you to compete with another woman for his love, he's sending you the loudest message you can ever receive. He doesn't love you, and he doesn't value your heart. You are expendable and replaceable, and if he happens to meet a third woman he believes is better than you, he will cut you off and replace you with her. The saga will continue, with or without you. You should get out now and spare your heart so you can love again when you meet a real man who knows your worth. Love is valuable, but you won't have to play a child's game to get it. The man for you will see your worth, respect your value, and make you his one and only woman. If competition is on the menu, leave the table.

Sheri's Perspective

I am the competitive type in almost everything I do. If I am running outside and someone is coming up behind me, I will nearly kill myself to win in a race that the other person doesn't even know we are competing in. If we are playing couples' minute-to-win-it games, I go all out and try my best to win, and I won't be happy if I lose. I am still working on the sore loser part of it, but that's for another book, lol! But one area I won't compete in is relationships.

You are enough. A lot of times in these types of relationships, women are broken down to a point where they begin to question themselves and think that if they can do something better, it'll keep a man faithful. I assure you that if a man is looking to cheat, he will. You can have a Jennifer Lopez body and Oprah money and still be cheated on.

A mature man will leave the relationship and explain to you why things won't work rather than cheating on you. Of course, women aren't perfect and can be disrespectful or do other things that can cause a man to want to leave, but that shouldn't cause a man to cheat. A man who cheats is trying to maintain a relationship while fulfilling other outside lusts without any regard for his relationship.

You are enough and deserve more. If a man makes you feel like you aren't enough in a relationship, that relationship is not for you. Be okay walking away from a situation if it's toxic or devalues you in any way. When a man makes you compete for his love, it becomes a game to him. Your livelihood, self-worth, and love are all pieces in the game. Don't allow yourself to be played. Love yourself enough to walk away.

A WOMAN'S INFLUENCE

I hope this book spoke to you in ways you expected it to. Please understand that trying to convey a message this deep is far from easy. Please forgive me for anything that may not be completely clear. I repeated myself a few times in the book because those thoughts are important to remember. A woman's influence is much bigger than influencing a man. It actually starts with influencing herself. That is why some of the chapters aren't speaking to influencing a man but instead reminding you of your strength and worth as a woman. As you read the book a second time, I'm sure completely different messages will jump out at you. It's hard to take in this much information all at once, so use only what you feel you need. As a man, I really want to convey the message to women that you don't have to settle, compromise, or chase a man. I want women to understand that you can be strong and loving at the same time. To love unconditionally doesn't mean you have to be weak or allow a man to mistreat you. You can stand your ground with complete respect and self-love.

We've been conditioned to see things based on what we are or where we are. I hope my tone isn't too blunt for you. If it was, please realize that it's because of how I was raised and direct messages were all I received. In the moments when your mouth dropped open, pay close attention to that point, because there is a message there. The parts that I drag out and overexplain, that's intentional as well. I want you to really feel the weight of the message and how I see it as a man. It isn't easy for men and women to fully understand each other's perspectives. We are different beings, created uniquely. I urge you as a woman to try to grasp where I'm coming from without being offended. I urge you as a man to try to grasp where my wife is coming from without being offended. We are only one couple. I can't say that our way will work for everyone or that it's the only way. We know that's not the case. All I can say is that God made a way for us to be in this position and add our story to the overall narrative around relationships. I look forward to connecting with you at a seminar or somewhere down the line to dive deeper into the topics we've covered in the book. That's all from me. I'll let my queen close out the book with a message from her heart. Thank you for taking the time out of your busy life to give our book a chance. Talk soon!

Sheri's Closing Remarks

A woman has so much strength and power in life and love. And that power is in the form of influence. That influence can be used for good or bad. It's your choice. In order to use that influence, you have to develop it. Developing it starts with learning to be alone and finding happiness during that time. It's about setting standards and understanding your worth. You are deserving of a happy, healthy relationship, and you don't have to settle. Learn to walk away from anything that is toxic.

Once in a relationship, use your influence to uplift, encourage, and inspire. Your partner is your teammate; work together, and don't compete. Figure out ways to communicate effectively, and treat each other with respect. I hope this book encourages you to never settle for less than you deserve.